Penguin Critical Studies

The Return of the Nati

Dr Joseph Garver wrote his thes
Edinburgh, and he has also done research or lectured at universities in Ireland,
Finland, Saudi Arabia, the West Bank and the United States. Now a freelance
writer and tutor in London, he is married and has a son and daughter.

Penguin Critical Studies
Advisory Editors:
Stephen Coote and Bryan Loughrey

Thomas Hardy

The Return of the Native

Joseph Garver

Penguin Books

Penguin Books, 27 Wrights Lane, London W8 5TZ (Publishing and Editorial)
and Harmondsworth, Middlesex, England (Distribution and Warehouse)
Viking Penguin Inc., 40 West 23rd Street, New York, New York 10010, USA
Penguin Books Australia Ltd, Ringwood, Victoria, Australia
Penguin Books Canada Ltd, 2801 John Street, Markham, Ontario, Canada L3R 1B4
Penguin Books (NZ) Ltd, 182–190 Wairau Road, Auckland 10, New Zealand

First published 1988

Filmset in Monophoto Times
Made and printed in Great Britain by
Richard Clay Ltd, Bungay, Suffolk

The lines from 'No Second Troy' taken from *The Collected Poems of W. B. Yeats* reprinted
by permission of A. P. Watt Ltd. on behalf of Michael B. Yeats and Macmillan London Ltd.

For Sue Estermann

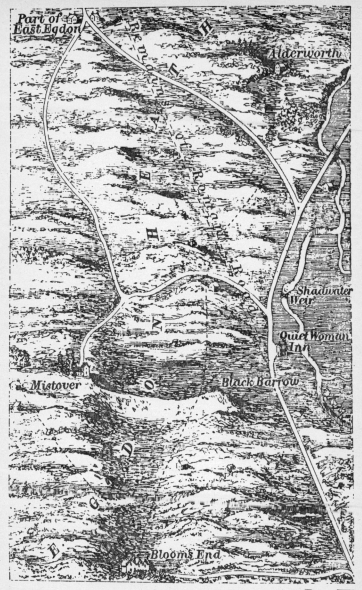

Hardy's own map of the scene of *The Return of the Native*. This map appeared in the first edition (1878) of the novel, in which the barrow dominating the landscape was called Black Barrow, not Rainbarrow.

Contents

Preface: The Return of Thomas Hardy 11

1. Biographical Introduction: The Native of Wessex 15
   Hardy's Early Development 15
   The Sense of Place 16
   The Prototype of Hardy's Fatalism 19
   The Implications of Caste 21
   Professional Aspirations 24
   London and the Apprenticeship in Literature 25
   The Early Novels 27
   The Genesis of *The Return of the Native* 36
   The Ur-Novel 37
   Published Versions of *The Return of the Native* 40
   Autobiographical Implications in *The Return of the Native* 44

2. *The Return of the Native* and Victorian Thought 50
   The Climate of Doubt 51
   The Pains of Agnosticism 53
   The Disappearance of God 55
   The Rejection of Meliorism 57
   The Implications of Darwinism 58
   The Conflict of 'Hellenism' and 'Hebraism' 63
   Ethical and Aesthetic Views of Life 65
   The Influence of Walter Pater's Aestheticism 67
   'The Ache of Modernism' 73

3. Plot, Structure and Form in *The Return of the Native* 75
   Background to Hardy's Conception of Plot 75
   Levels of Plot in *The Return of the Native* 79
   Unity of Action in the Realistic Plot 81
     Book I 81
     Book II 84
     Book III 85
     Book IV 87

Critical Studies: The Return of the Native

Book V	90
Book VI	93
Thematic Unity	95
Characterization in the Realistic Plot	98
Character Analyses	101
Setting and Realism in *The Return of the Native*	106
Point of View and Voice	111
The Tragic Level of Plot	114
Tragic Characterization in *The Return of the Native*	117
The Mythic Level of Plot	121
Eustacia as Mythic Victim	123
Bibliography	127

Preface: The Return of Thomas Hardy

The Return of the Native (1878), Hardy's seventh novel, was his first great tragic novel, anticipating *The Mayor of Casterbridge* (1886), *Tess of the d'Urbervilles* (1891) and *Jude the Obscure* (1895). When he began work on it, probably in the winter of 1876, in the quiet little north-Dorset town of Sturminster Newton, Hardy was already known as the author of *Under the Greenwood Tree* (1872), *A Pair of Blue Eyes* (1873) and the best-selling *Far from the Madding Crowd* (1874). However, the pastoral and elegiac charm of these earlier successes – notwithstanding the cruelly ironic death of the heroine in *A Pair of Blue Eyes* – had hardly prepared readers for this sombre seventh novel and its central vision of an implacable Destiny looming darkly, like Rainbarrow on Egdon Heath, over the natives of the earth. 'The reader found himself taken farther from the madding crowd than ever', *The Times* observed; and *The Athenaeum* pronounced Hardy's latest novel 'distinctly inferior to anything of his we have yet read'. Yet the reviews were not entirely condemnatory. More often they showed uncertainty and self-contradiction, as well they might before this astonishingly original and powerful work. No less astonishing was the appearance of such a work first in the sheep's clothing of an illustrated 'family-magazine' serial and then in the conventional three-volume dress of the circulating-library novel.

We can now see that *The Return* was definitely a new departure in Hardy's career as a novelist. It was first of all a highly deliberate – and risky – move from the quasi-pastoral mode, where Hardy had scored his greatest successes thus far, to the tragic. Not the least remarkable aspects of *The Return* are the implicit challenge of comparison with Aeschylus and Shakespeare and the metaphoric transformation of novelistic setting into dramatic unity of place and time, the abiding heath becoming a stage on which characters enter, exit, spy on one another, reproach one another, soliloquize, suffer and die. Virtually all the action takes place within view of that gigantic grave, Rainbarrow; and the main action is restricted in time to the traditional cycle of a year and a day. Moreover, this figurative observance of the Aristotelian unities was but part of the general strengthening of integrity and purpose which distinguishes *The Return* from Hardy's previous novels. He was now clearly prepared to sacrifice commercial success in order to achieve an aesthetic advance; to show himself, to rearrange some phrases from his often-quoted letter to Leslie Stephen, not merely 'a good hand at a serial', but 'a great stickler for the proper artistic balance of the completed work'.

However, as its highly evocative title suggests, *The Return of the Native* was also a reaffirmation and a rediscovery; a thematic 'return' for its author. Hardy's immediately preceding novel, *The Hand of Ethelberta: A Comedy in Chapters* (1876), had been a largely unconvincing venture into the comedy of manners, that middle-class genre in which satirical novelists like Thackeray and Trollope excelled. Now in his seventh novel Hardy was to turn back to the starker vision of life inherent, for him, in his native landscape and mores. In effect, the author, like the persona of Wordsworth's *The Prelude* (1850), was to return to himself, but with heightened insight, sublimation and control.

More than most Victorian authors, Hardy had difficulty in finding a balance in his writing between the subjective or autobiographical and the objective or impersonal. Consequently, authorial voice, tone and point of view were often problematic, especially in his early fiction. In what was evidently a mistake, he had written his unpublishable first novel, *The Poor Man and the Lady*, in first-person narration, even inscribing 'By the Poor Man' on the title page and naming its hero 'Strong' synonymously with his own name. After thus blatantly revealing himself, Hardy, in virtually all his subsequent fiction, adhered to third-person narration, apparently as part of a method to control point of view and the strained subjectivity that had still intruded in his second novel, *Desperate Remedies* (1871), and to some extent in *A Pair of Blue Eyes* and *Ethelberta*. (Hardy even dictated his autobiography in the third person and attributed its authorship to his second wife, though this was partly a ruse intended to forestall biographical probing into his private life.) In *Far from the Madding Crowd* he had created a convincing modern Arcadia – where 'God's above the devil yet!' – but at the expense of limiting voice and point of view and of excluding much of himself from the novel.

In returning to himself in his fateful seventh novel, Hardy was finally able to imbue Arcadia with his own tragic vision of life, creating in the process the mythic realm of Wessex, which is first realized in *The Return*. In the dark heart of Wessex – Egdon Heath – Hardy was able to objectify and dramatize his own illusions and preoccupations, which through this act of aesthetic distancing blend into the epochal and the universal. The disappearance of God, Darwinian fears of racial decline, social alienation and the philistine biases of caste, the abyss of the deracinated personality, the Kierkegaardian antilogy of the ethical and the aesthetic, the treacheries of Romantic nostalgia – all of these dilemmas have their objective correlatives on the heath, and most of them continue to haunt us today as they once did the Victorians.

But if *The Return* was a kind of symbolic autobiography, its title page bore, not the blatant inscription 'By the Native', but a gracefully detached statement of emotion, namely a quotation from Keats's roundelay 'O Sorrow'. For in *The Return* Hardy transcended his old awkwardness with voice and point of view by creating an effect of simultaneity, as if the point of view were now both within and external to the story; as if, in terms of Aristotelian rhetoric, *ethos* (ideal detachment) and *pathos* (subjective emotion) were now indistinguishable. The narrator's voice contrives to be both idiosyncratic and impersonal, helping to project that peculiarly 'bifocal' vision of scene, event and character noted by a recent writer on Hardy, Ian Gregor. Description and setting in *The Return*, as in the famous opening evocation of Egdon Heath, reflect the same subtle reconciliation of antitheses. The heath is real, from its chartable topography to the smallest visual, aural and tactile detail; but at the same time its presence is as overwhelmingly metaphoric as Ahab's white whale or the moorland manor-house, Wuthering Heights. As D. H. Lawrence insisted, the heath is both womb and grave; both mother and layer-out of the dead. The unimpressionable face of 'haggard Egdon' mirrors Time himself that 'destroyer of his own romances', in the words of *Tess of the d'Urbervilles*. But whereas the sense of place in a Wessex novel like *Tess* is panoramic, in *The Return* it is dioramic, focusing inwards, ever more intensely, on the map of infinity, through the heart of Wessex, Egdon Heath, to the omphalos, Rainbarrow. Here, as we gradually realize the futility of the doomed Eustacia's telescope and hourglass, we come finally to grasp Hardy's achievement in localizing the eternal.

None of Hardy's other novels is more ambitious in conception, none went through a more protracted gestation and delivery, and none has been more mercilessly dissected by critics. Yet *The Return* holistically transcends its alleged inconsistencies and shortcomings; and the myriad, often contradictory analyses and critical verdicts bear witness to its enduring vitality. At any rate, hostile criticism, misapprehension and some shortfall in achievement were the price paid by Hardy for his innovation and experimentation with form. In short, we can see Hardy making himself into a major novelist in *The Return*. It was this first brilliant exploration of the tragic mythos of Wessex that made possible the later, even greater novels. When *Far from the Madding Crowd* had begun to appear, as an anonymous serial, readers at first took it for a new novel by George Eliot. No such mistake could have occurred with *The Return.* Its voice was distinctive, if not at first fully appreciated; and its more prescient readers could recognize a new creator of the novel to rank with Eliot, Dickens, Thackeray, Trollope and Meredith.

Hardy's work is related, more than that of any other Victorian novelist, to the author's native origins; and of all Hardy's novels, *The Return* probes deepest into those origins. Therefore, we begin our study with the biographical background. A basic familiarity with *The Return* is assumed throughout, but readers who wish to refresh their memories may turn first to Chapter 3, in which the plot is reviewed in detail. Since there are various editions of *The Return* available, quotations will be identified by chapter only. For example, the citation (I:ii) following a quotation means that it is taken from Book I, Chapter 2. Secondary sources are listed in the Bibliography.

1. Biographical Introduction: The Native of Wessex

Hardy's Early Development

Hardy was born in 1840 in a cottage in the hamlet of Higher Bock-hampton, which is in the parish of Stinsford about three miles east of Dorchester, the county town of Dorset, in that part of southwestern England traditionally known as the West Country. His mother, Jemima, had been a maid and a cook; moreover, as children, she and her sisters had suffered the degradation of official pauperism on parish support. However, his father was a self-employed stonemason who owned his own house, a sizeable, two-storey cottage. Virtually independent of squire and landlord, Hardy's father enjoyed a status corresponding roughly to that of the old yeoman class. He prospered, and by the time of his son's majority he was a master-mason employing several workmen. Yet he seems to have had little worldly ambition in comparison with the strong-minded Jemima; Hardy always considered his mother to have been the dominant influence on himself. Although probably neither of Hardy's parents was completely literate, both were remarkably self-educated. Jemima, if she never learned to write properly, had acquired from her own mother a love of reading, particularly Dante's *Divine Comedy*. She taught Hardy to read before he was four; and when he went to his first school at the age of eight she presented him with three works quite representative of the range of contemporary taste: Dryden's translation (1697) of Virgil's *Aeneid*; Dr Johnson's *Rasselas* (1759); and Saint-Pierre's Rosseauist fable, *Paul and Virginia* (1787). From his father he inherited a love of music. Hardy's father and paternal grandfather had been pillars of the Stinsford Church instrumental choir, which is portrayed lovingly in *Under the Greenwood Tree*, Stinsford figuring there as 'Mellstock'; and Hardy's father never allowed work to interfere with music. Hardy himself was as precocious a musician as he was a reader; and, although the barrel-organ had ousted the traditional church choirs by the time of his childhood, he regularly fiddled at local festivities.

Hardy was an unusually observant, impressionable and reflective child – a likely 'ghost-seer', as such a child was sometimes called. This personality was the result of physical delicacy as well as of his mother's desire to keep him apart from 'common' children and instil in him a seriousness beyond his years. The child kept by the chimney-corner became not only an avid reader, but also a listener to adult conversation and a connoisseur of the often grim local folklore. Moreover, his precocity as a fiddler gave him entrée to adult functions and much scope for spectatorship. Indeed, the local dances, at which both Hardy and his father fiddled, sometimes turned orgiastic; no doubt their febrile atmosphere is recalled in the August 'gipsying' in *The Return*, at which Eustacia and Wildeve inhale the 'Pagan' atmosphere and experience their fatal loosening of inhibition. Doubtless, too, the sexual frankness which frequently troubled Hardy's editors and reviewers derived from the early years at Higher Bockhampton.

Thus, despite his early introversion, Hardy witnessed much of Dorset folk-life; and he also came into contact with local life as a churchgoer and later as a Sunday School teacher, even being called on by the girls in his class to write their love letters. He was present, at the age of ten, at what was probably the last traditional harvest supper in Stinsford, an experience drawn upon in *Far from the Madding Crowd*. Still, observation is not the same as participation; and recent biography emphasizes Hardy's abnormal introversion and the detached observation which seems to be characteristic both of his formative years and of the voice of his novels. In any event, Hardy was born just in time to absorb and record – at whatever personal cost – the atmosphere and significance of a way of life soon to disappear forever.

The Sense of Place

Although the railway reached Dorchester in 1847 and other radical changes were only a few decades in the future, the countryside of Hardy's childhood was still backward-looking; remarkably unaffected by improvement and industrialization; and, of course, dialect-speaking. The Hardy cottage stood on the edge of the bleak heathlands which then stretched eastward from Stinsford to Bournemouth on the Hampshire border. In keeping with the atmosphere of remoteness and even desolation, the landscape was marked by the remains of vanished races and fallen civilizations. Within sight of Hardy's birthplace was Rainbarrows, a group of three Celtic tumuli on a hill overlooking the track of the Roman road running north from Dorchester (itself prehistoric in origin) to Salisbury. Just outside Dorchester ('Casterbridge') was Maumbury Rings, the sinister ruins of a Roman amphitheatre used more recently as a place of execution and a duelling-ground; and two miles southwest of the ancient town lay the vast earthworks called

Maiden Castle, whose last garrison had died resisting a Roman assault two millennia before.

In such a countryside, folk memories were long; customs and beliefs persistent; and even conjuring and witchcraft not unknown. Cases of 'witch-pricking', such as that inflicted upon Eustacia, were recorded in Dorset as late as the 1880s. Local anti-Catholicism, shown in the burning in effigy of the Pope and Cardinal Wiseman in Maumbury Rings on Guy Fawkes Day, 1850 – a rowdy ritual witnessed by Hardy – derived from traditions of Monmouth's Rebellion in 1685, when the Puritans of the West Country – among them Hardy's maternal ancestors – had risen with the Duke of Monmouth against James II, the last Roman Catholic monarch of Britain. It had not been forgotten how, after Monmouth's rout at the Battle of Sedgemoor in Somerset, Tory troopers had scoured the moors and heaths, Judge Jeffreys had held his 'Bloody Assizes', and Dorset men had rotted on gibbets in Maumbury Rings. Hence the vigour of the Dorset celebration of the destruction of that Popish arch-villain Guy Fawkes, the ritual dominating the opening scenes of *The Return*. Moreover, the presence at that Rainbarrow bonfire of Grandfer Cantle, the vainglorious veteran of the 'Bang-up Locals', reflects another local tradition, the Napoleonic invasion scare along the Dorset coast, when corps of volunteers had mustered, beacons had been prepared on hilltops, and 'Boney' had become a local bugbear, occasionally even displacing the Turkish Knight in the mummers' play. As a child, Hardy saw the remains of the beacon guard's hut on Rainbarrows.

His native landscape and its associations seem to have induced very early in Hardy that profound sense of place which characterizes all his writings. Cognate with this *genius loci*, apparently, was a nostalgic retrospection; a sense of sadness in the passage of time and the imminence of change, and a reluctance to enter the great bustling world beyond Stinsford or even to grow up. Such attitudes were stimulated or confirmed through the young Hardy's reading of Romantic and pre-Romantic poetry such as Gray's 'Elegy in a Country Church Yard' (1751), a line of which yielded the title *Far from the Madding Crowd*. Nostalgic meditation is already evident in Hardy's earliest composition, 'Domicilium' ('Home'), possibly written in his sixteenth year. This markedly Wordsworthian poem first describes the fertile side of the family cottage, which had been built by Hardy's great-grandfather, then the heath side, and finally the *past* appearance of the cottage. Here are the last two parts of 'Domicilium':

Behind, the scene is wilder. Heath and furze

> *Are everything that seems to grow and thrive*
> *Upon uneven ground. A stunted thorn*
> *Stands here and there, indeed; and from a pit*
> *An oak uprises, springing from a seed*
> *Dropped by some bird a hundred years ago.*
>   *In days bygone –*
> *Long gone – my father's mother, who is now*
> *Blest with the blest, would take me out to walk.*
> *At such a time I once inquired of her*
> *How looked the spot when first she settled here.*
> *The answer I remember. 'Fifty years*
> *Have passed since then, my child, and change has marked*
> *The face of all things. Yonder garden-plots*
> *And orchards were uncultivated slopes*
> *O'ergrown with bramble bushes, furze, and thorn:*
> *That road a narrow path shut in by ferns,*
> *Which, almost trees, obscured the passer-by.*
>
> *Our house stood quite alone, and those tall firs*
> *And beeches were not planted. Snakes and efts* [newts or lizards]
> *Swarmed in the summer days, and nightly bats*
> *Would fly about our bedrooms. Heathcroppers* [wild ponies]
> *Lived on the hills, and were our only friends;*
> *So wild it was when first we settled here.'*

In its evocation of place, stimulation of feeling by natural detail, and retrospective assumption, this early poem not only anticipates Hardy's mature powers of description – perhaps the embryo of Egdon Heath can even be discerned here – but also demonstrates the seminal influence of his native surroundings.

'Domicilium' also anticipates another characteristic of the Wessex novels, the basing of imagined scenes and action upon 'real' scenery and background, whether landscape, natural objects, landmarks or buildings. And the case in point here is *The Return*. Even a limited knowledge of Stinsford enables one to see distinct correspondences with the setting of the novel. Obviously, Rainbarrows, from which Hardy's father – like Eustacia – used to sweep the heath with a naval telescope, inspired the fictional Rainbarrow, the original three mounds being transformed into one grander barrow. Egdon Heath itself, as Hardy says in his preface to *The Return*, 'united or typified' several local heaths into a composite portrait of wilderness. Indeed, Hardy's map of the scene of *The Return*, which was printed as a frontispiece in the first edition, is clearly, though not exactly, based on the topography of the Higher Bockhampton area (though Hardy partially disguised his parish by disorientating the compass directions and by originally naming the tumulus 'Blackbarrow'). Even the originals of such minutiae as the Devil's Bellows – the wind-blasted copse near Clym's cottage at Alderworth – and Oker's Pool – the tiny pond from which Johnny Nunsuch unavailingly fetches water for the stricken Mrs Yeobright – have been identified. More significantly, Hardy's map and other evidence indicate that Blooms-End is based at least in part on Higher Bockhampton, inevitably suggesting some correspondence between the Yeobright home, also called Blooms-End, and the Hardy cottage. We shall take up the autobiographical implications of these remarkable correspondences later. For the moment, let us only note that the powerful evocation of spirit of place in *The Return* evidently derives directly from the author's powerful childhood identification with a metaphoric 'domicilium' encompassing home, family, community and landscape.

The Prototype of Hardy's Fatalism

The almost hallucinatory intensity of visualization characteristic of many of the scenes of *The Return* may also derive from memories of childhood perceptions. In Hardy's isolated childhood – as in that of the Brontës twenty years earlier in their moorland parsonage – unusual events or impressions of personal life seemed to take on, either in actual experience or in retrospect, a larger-than-life or phantasmal quality. One such preternatural event was the appearance of a serpent in the infant Hardy's cradle. Another was his sole act of gambling when, the only child present, he won a raffle for a hen by amazingly throwing a pair-royal (three of a kind) – as does the simpleton Christian in *The Return*. Hardy was also struck by the winged skull on a tomb in Stinsford Church, a fascination recalled in the uncanny optical illusion described in the opening of his novelette *An Indiscretion in the Life of an Heiress* (1878). A mood of reluctance to grow older and face the 'afar-noised World' which struck Hardy as he sheltered from the rain under fronds is recalled in his poem 'Childhood among the Ferns'. Of course, an abiding influence on the child's imagination was the surrounding heath itself, which, with its moths, heath-bells, birds, crystals, 'Druidical' stones and flint arrow-heads, was a source of beauty and wonder. Yet after nightfall it became, like Egdon Heath, 'the home of strange phantoms . . . the hitherto unrecognized original of those wild regions of obscurity which are vaguely felt to be compassing us about in midnight dreams of flight and disaster' (I:i).

19

As these recollections suggest, the dark side of Hardy's imagination also appears to have developed early, always stimulated by local history and folklore. In addition to ghost stories, the child would have heard tales of the murderous mantraps set for poachers; tales of the brutal press-gangs; tales of smugglers – the Hardy cottage itself had been used as a hiding place for contraband spirits; and accounts of gruesome executions, such as that of a girl burned at the stake in 1706 in Maumbury Rings, or the barbaric hangings, witnessed by Hardy's father, of starving peasants suspected of rick-burning. From his mother Hardy heard of a girl buried as a suicide with a stake driven through her body. Nor were all such things in the past. As a child, Hardy himself had known a lad who starved to death: it was only after the repeal of the Corn Laws in 1846 that the price of bread was reduced sufficiently to obviate starvation. Moreover, at the age of sixteen Hardy witnessed from just below the scaffold the hanging at Dorchester Gaol of Martha Browne, who, like the girl burned in Maumbury Rings, had been convicted of her husband's murder. He never forgot the striking figure of this victim of justice.

Quite early, probably, such annals and observations of the dark side of Dorset life became assimilated into an implicit world-view of pessimism and fatalism, though Hardy always insisted later that he was a realist, not a pessimist. No doubt such an attitude to life reflects the native Calvinism and its central tenets of innate depravity, predestination and eternal damnation – the ancestral ideology that during Monmouth's Rebellion had inspired West Countrymen armed with scythes and sickles to engage royal dragoons in battle. Hardy most strikingly introduced popular Calvinism, in the form of Evangelicalism, in *Tess of the d'Urbervilles*, though the flames of hell are also present, metaphorically, in the imagery applied to Egdon Heath in the *The Return*. The enthusiast encountered by Tess, who paints in red a 'tex' like THY, DAMNATION, SLUMBERETH, NOT, on every wall, gate and stile he passes, had probably also been encountered by Hardy. Jemima Hardy's passion for Dante's *Divine Comedy* no doubt had its source in a similar penchant for hellfire.

However, Hardy's fatalistic vision also derived from a folk pessimism going deeper than Calvinism; from an almost pagan sense of blind destiny before which even piety is helpless. Having suffered bitter deprivation in her own childhood, Hardy's mother would have encouraged such an implicit fatalism. Jemima intimated that one was to work hard and strive for self-improvement, but one was not to attract Nemesis by showing pride in success. She severely rebuked her son for his single indulgence in the devil's game of dicing, an indulgence all the more dangerous because his throw had been so lucky. Sexual attraction was another snare; Jemima was even opposed to her children's getting married (of her four children only Thomas himself *did* marry). Instead of jeopardizing themselves in such a lottery, they were to live together in pairs, brother and sister, for mutual protection. 'Mother's notion (and also mine)', Hardy noted in 1870, is 'that a figure stands in our van with arms uplifted, to knock us back from any pleasant prospect we indulge in as probable'.

The Implications of Caste

Another important influence in Hardy's development was class consciousness. As an artisan, an owner of real estate – however modest in extent – and an employer of other workmen – on however small a scale – Hardy's father was separated by a division of caste from the labourers, shepherds and poor tenantry who constituted the peasantry proper or 'heath-folk' as they are called in *The Return*. However, by similar criteria of income, property, family background and education, the Hardys – artisans by calling for at least four generations – were inferior socially to the local middle class and gentility. With allowance for the provinciality of Dorset, the 'middle class' here included sufficiently well-to-do farmers, tradesmen and merchants; retired Navy and Army officers; and professional men such as the clergy, doctors and lawyers. Strictly speaking, the gentility included only the landed gentry or 'county families', i.e. the owners of hereditary estates, who might even inherit titles with their lands. But in practice there was much overlapping of the middle class and the gentility. Thus Captain Vye, retired on half-pay from the Royal Navy, and Mrs Yeobright, the daughter of a curate and widow of a farmer, are the gentility of Egdon. Above all in the parish was the 'squire', an informal title usually applied to the major landowner. Certainly, the obsession with social status in *The Return* – with Mrs Yeobright and Eustacia bitterly disputing precedence – is entirely typical of the society known by Hardy.

In the Stinsford of Hardy's childhood, the squire was the owner of the Kingston Maurward manor near Higher Bockhampton, from which Hardy's father occasionally received commissions for building work. The squire's wife sponsored a parish school, run by the National Society for Promoting the Education of the Poor in the Principles of the Established Church; and it was this humbling 'National' institution which Hardy attended as his first school from 1848 to 1850. In fact, as a strikingly precocious scholar, he became the pet of the patroness; and recent biography emphasizes the passionate devotion which the child showed to her as the germ of a major theme in Hardy's fiction, namely attraction between a lower-class man and an upper-class woman, as in *The Poor Man and the Lady*. No doubt Hardy had his first experiences both of being patronized and of being snubbed at Kingston Maurward.

Hardy suffered throughout his life from feelings of social inferiority. The ineluctable, if not always definable, barriers of class that limited freedom in education, employment, profession, social life and marriage also played a part in the development of his fatalistic inclinations. Furthermore, in the society of a provincial town like Dorchester, no less than in a tradition-bound parish like Stinsford, the sense of caste was even stronger than in early Victorian society in general. In old age Hardy still recalled with bitterness how, when his parents paid for his apprenticeship to an architect, the vicar of Stinsford had rebuked Hardy and Jemima from the pulpit for presuming to aspire to the middle class. Even after Hardy had become an internationally recognized author, there were still people in Dorchester who regarded him as socially beneath their notice. Indeed, the burghers of Dorchester could not bring themselves to offer him the Freedom of the Borough until after he had received the Order of Merit from George V in 1910.

Hardy also had before him the spectre of social regression or loss of caste, such as that Venn suffers in becoming a reddleman – an itinerant seller of dye for sheep – in *The Return*. Those in the position of Hardy's father, at the apex of the lower classes, even if they had the prospect of seeing a succeeding generation ascend to the middle class also faced the ever-present possibility of falling back, through just a little bad luck, into the lower depths. In *Far from the Madding Crowd* one inexperienced sheepdog reduces Farmer Oak overnight to hireling shepherd. Among Hardy's close relatives on both his father's and his mother's sides were 'work-folk'; and his mother herself, as already mentioned, had experienced the dreaded fall to pauperism. Always in the abyss yawned the gates of the workhouse, which swallows Fanny Robin in *Far from the Madding Crowd*.

No less troublesome to an aspirant to middle-class status were the multifarious embarrassments arising from questions of class identity. For despite appearances the social hierarchy was not really stable; its rigidity was becoming more and more qualified by confusion of caste lines, though, naturally, losing caste was always easier than gaining it. For example, when Hardy was a young architectural assistant living in Higher Bockhampton, a middle-class friend was uncertain whether to put the significant courtesy tag *Esqre.* after Hardy's name on envelopes. A similar embarrassment occurs at Blooms-End: is Venn to have his tea in the kitchen or in the parlour? Moreover, the yeoman class, from which Hardy's father had sprung, was rapidly becoming obsolete; and a new pushy class of rootless, self-made men was beginning to appear. The potential embarrassment in such discontinuity of the generations is illustrated in a scene in *The Hand of Ethelberta*, in which the heroine, having won her way into the upper circles, finds herself, as a guest, decorously waited on at table by her own father, the butler. And thus we have Captain Vye's commonsense solution to Clym's vocational dilemma: he should have become a farmer like his father.

Because of his concern with his social respectability and his self-de-fensive punctiliousness in observing social decorum, Hardy has himself been accused of snobbery. But he was never a social climber; and, though a self-made man himself, Hardy seems to have felt little identity with the rising meritocracy. At the same time, he supposed himself to lack gentle-manly presence and acquirements. Such feelings of inadequacy were doubtless exacerbated by his first social encounters with middle-class girls. Here Stephen Smith's embarrassed ignorance of horsemanship before the rector's daughter in *A Pair of Blue Eyes* reflects Hardy's own experiences with his dashingly equestrian fiancée, Emma Gifford, who was the daughter of a solicitor and sister-in-law of a rector. Again, the class barrier partly explains why Hardy directed much of his courtship within his own family; when he met Emma, he seems to have been informally engaged to his maternal first cousin, Tryphena Sparks.

Ultimately, Hardy's social attitudes seem to have become dominated not only by nostalgia for the vanishing yeoman class, but also by the conviction that his own family represented genealogical and racial de-cadence. He persuaded himself that the Stinsford Hardys – unlike the Hands, his mother's family – were not simply of indigenous, Saxon, yeoman stock, but were in fact the lineal descendants of a fifteenth-century Norman seigneur, Clement le Hardy, of Jersey. Hardy professed to see in his family as well as in himself symptoms of the lineal decline characteristic of 'an old family of spent social energies', as he put it in his autobiography. The telltale signs of this decline were his father's inherent lack of ambition and his own failure 'to take advantage of the many worldly opportunities that his popularity and esteem as an author afforded him'. Such a personal myth seems to underlie the recurrent theme in Hardy's fiction of the decay of a noble, Norman line and its supersession by a modern, vulgar stock. Another form of familial decline seems to be inherent in Clym's 'wrinkled' mind and withdrawal from the world. Nevertheless, Hardy took a melancholy pride in his supposed descent from ancestral grandeur – he even considered adding 'le' to his name – and he thus resented all the more the bourgeois snobs of Dorchester. 'Ours was also a county family if they only knew,' he complained. But we can finally see in this obsession with genealogy and hereditary doom another aspect of Hardy's fatalism.

Professional Aspirations

To return to Hardy's childhood, it was undoubtedly his spirited mother who first instilled class consciousness and social ambition in him. Jemima soon became jealous of the squire's wife's patronizing of her talented son; and in 1850 she removed Hardy from that lady's charity school and sent him to a Nonconformist schoolmaster in Dorchester, with whom Hardy continued until the end of his formal schooling in 1856. However, this change, which led to a breach with the squire's wife and loss of work for Hardy's father at Kingston Maurward, was ostensibly made for academic reasons, the new school having a reputation for both practical and higher subjects. Jemima paid extra for Latin, a sign of her ambition for her son. Here another incident in Hardy's fiction is relevant. In *The Woodlanders* (1887) Mr Melbury resolves to educate properly his daughter because of the shame he himself had suffered as a work-lad when the parson's son had demanded of him, 'Who dragged Whom round the walls of What?' Like Melbury, Jemima apparently saw education as the chief means to offset social disadvantage, especially the classical learning which not only held the key to self-assurance – and the key to Melbury's humiliating riddle – but was also the prerequisite for the professions. His study of Latin meant that Hardy was intended to do more than simply succeed his father as parish mason.

Evidently, the boy's physical delicacy and bookishness had originally suggested the possibility of a professional career; and his first choice of profession was the Church. But a proper career there required an Oxbridge degree, and obvious social and financial obstacles precluded university entrance for Hardy. Instead, the sixteen-year-old boy was articled for three years to the Dorchester architect John Hicks, who accepted a reduced fee of £40, thanks to the connections of Hardy's father in the building trade. Recognizing the opportunity to rise to at least the lower rung of the professional classes, Hardy applied himself to architecture, yet without abandoning either his classical studies or his dream of university and Church. With a tenacity like that of the protagonist of *Jude the Obscure*, Hardy in his spare time kept up his Latin and began to teach himself Greek. Again like Jude, Hardy enjoyed at least a physical proximity to ecclesiastical affairs, for Hicks's speciality was church restoration. Hardy was now also making his first attempts to write poetry, 'Domicilium' alone surviving from these early efforts.

Hardy was fortunate not only for the indulgence of Hicks, who was sympathetic to Hardy's self-education, but also in his friendship with Horace Moule, the son of a local vicar. Eight years Hardy's senior and a budding scholar and critic, Moule encouraged Hardy's literary study; indeed, although himself tortured by alcoholism, he acted intermittently as Hardy's counsellor until his suicide in 1873. Having attended both Oxford and Cambridge, Moule was Hardy's vital link with contemporary intellectual life, probably serving also as a partial model for Angel Clare in *Tess*. He was perhaps the only intimate friend Hardy ever had.

Hardy got on well with Hicks, who took him on as a regular assistant in 1860. However, he still lived off and on at the beloved cottage in Higher Bockhampton and remained partially dependent on his parents. By 1861, the year of his majority, Hardy was a competent architectural surveyor with special training in ecclesiastical design; and his parents hoped soon to see him fully launched. He certainly seemed well on his way to realizing his mother's ambition of a rise to at least lower-middle-class status. He had also advanced in the classics, yet he was still without a prospect of realizing his dream of university entrance. All in all, it was probably a compound of his own soaring hopes and his mother's more practical ambitions that sent Hardy to seek his fortune in the metropolis.

London and the Apprenticeship in Literature

The Hardy who arrived in London in April 1862, prudently armed with letters of introduction and a return ticket, was 'pink-faced' and countrified, speaking with a Dorset accent. Yet, as in his earlier throw with the dice, Hardy was extraordinarily lucky. He happily was referred to a well-established ecclesiastical architect, Arthur Blomfield, who needed an assistant with exactly his qualifications. Hardy rapidly established himself in Blomfield's office and threw away his return ticket. However, in the following five years in London, he advanced his literary as well as his architectural apprenticeship.

It was during the London years that Hardy caught up with the intellectual and cultural developments of his time. He heard Dickens's public readings. He frequented the theatre to see Shakespeare's plays, the opera and the many exhibitions that characterized this self-congratulatory period of Victorian culture. He haunted the National Gallery, studying the effects of allegory, perspective and chiaroscuro, which were to influence the descriptive technique of his novels, and acquiring that detailed knowledge of Renaissance painting that was to appear, sometimes rather obtrusively, in his fiction. Without abandoning his classical studies, Hardy was also pressing on with his reading not only of fashionable novelists like Trollope and Bulwer-Lytton, but also of the revolutionary authors of the time such as Ruskin, whose series, *Modern Painters* (1843–60), was remaking art criticism; Darwin, whose *On the Origin of Species* had appeared in 1859; T. H. Huxley, the formidable biologist who was smashing Darwin's critics; Comte, the founder of Positivism; and J. S. Mill, whose *On Liberty* (1859) Hardy virtually learnt by heart.

However, Hardy's biographers are embarrassed by these London years because so few details are known of his development and inner life during this momentous period, to which his autobiography devotes only a few vague pages. For example, it does not mention Eliza Nicholls, a lady's maid, to whom Hardy seems to have been engaged from 1863 to 1867. During the London years Hardy apparently not only gave up his hopes of university and Church, but also gradually lost his belief in Christianity and even in the existence of a beneficent deity, though he remained attached to the music and ritual of the Anglican liturgy. We can also infer that during these years he first conceived of writing as an alternative to architecture. His private study had now begun to encompass the principles of rhetoric as applied to prose style; and he was also writing poems of some maturity, though he could not interest editors in them.

1867 was a momentous year for Hardy. In that year he broke off his engagement to Eliza; suffered a decline in health; gave up his employment in London and returned to assist Hicks again in Dorchester; and began his first novel, *The Poor Man and the Lady.* Ostensibly Hardy's only reason for leaving London was to recover his health; but perhaps he was coming to realize that lack of social connections would limit his advancement as an architect in London. Even in Dorchester, however, lack of capital and social rank would be serious obstacles to his ever setting up independent practice. On the other hand, the possibility of becoming a professional writer or critic, which had exercised him in London, was even more uncertain. He had consulted Moule about whether to neglect architecture in favour of the Greek tragedians; and Moule, who himself scraped a bare living from reviewing and tutoring, had advised him to stick to architecture, which at least ensured a livelihood. In the end Hardy compromised, working part-time with Hicks while drafting his first novel.

The Early Novels

It is uncertain how Hardy finally came to choose the novel as the form of his first major creative effort: he always professed to find fiction aesthetically inferior to poetry. Presumably he saw the novel as at once the best-paid professional writing and the most suitable vehicle for his own self-expression. According to his autobiography, Hardy

considered that he knew fairly well both West-country life in its less explored recesses and the life of an isolated student cast upon the billows of London with no protection but his brains . . . The two contrasting experiences seemed to afford him abundant materials out of which to evolve a striking socialistic novel.

In any event, in July 1868 he submitted, on Moule's advice, *The Poor Man and the Lady* to the London publisher Alexander Macmillan.

Although Hardy later destroyed the manuscript, we can reconstruct from various sources the substance of the novel read by Macmillan. Its episodic story was narrated in the first person, supposedly in imitation of Defoe, by its protagonist, Will Strong, a young man of Dorset peasant stock. As a result of his promise as a child, Strong has been given schooling and architectural training by the local squire. However, when Strong and the squire's beautiful daughter Geraldine fall in love, the squire angrily forbids them to meet. Banished, Strong becomes an architect's assistant in London and a political radical. In London Geraldine hears Strong address a rally of working men; later the lovers meet at a concert. When Strong attempts to call at her father's town house, the squire has him thrown out and returns Geraldine to Dorset where a suitable marriage has been arranged for her. Strong follows, meets Geraldine in church on the eve of her wedding, and persuades her to marry him instead. She does so, but then she abruptly falls ill and dies in the squire's house. Strong designs her memorial without charging the squire, who is pleased at the saving. 'The story was, in fact,' in Hardy's words, 'a sweeping dramatic satire of the squirearchy and nobility, London society, the vulgarity of the middle class, modern Christianity, church-restoration, and political and domestic morals in general.'

It says much for Hardy's untutored powers as a writer that such an obviously objectionable story should have been considered at all by a reputable publisher. However, while recognizing that the crudeness and relentlessness of its social criticism made *The Poor Man* unpublishable – at least by his firm – Macmillan was impressed enough by this beginner's novel to take great pains in assessing its strengths and weaknesses. Indeed, he seems to have treated Hardy with the consideration due to an author of great potential. Moreover, he introduced Hardy to another established publishing firm, Chapman & Hall. The result was one of the great encounters of literary history, for Chapman & Hall's reader was George Meredith, whose sequence of poems, *Modern Love* (1862), had already influenced Hardy's own verse. Himself the grandson of a tailor, Meredith knew only too well the class prejudice which Hardy meant to expose. Meredith also knew – as Hardy still did not – the power wielded by reviewers. At their memorable meeting, Meredith warned Hardy that if he published *The Poor Man and the Lady*, 'the press would be about his ears like hornets', and his future as an author would be in jeopardy. Instead, Meredith advised him to put aside *The Poor Man* and 'attempt a novel with a purely artistic purpose', subordinating social criticism to plot development.

Although Hardy finally accepted that *The Poor Man* was best left unpublished, he had good reason to feel strongly encouraged. With renewed vigour he set to work to write a novel along the lines suggested by Meredith. Fortunately, his health had been completely restored by his native air; and the *genius loci* seemed, like a muse, to inspire him anew. Fortunately, too, he had enough income from occasional architectural jobs to support his writing. Hardy must also have been invigorated by the company of his attractive young cousin, Tryphena Sparks. However, he was soon to find a new romance in the remote hamlet of St Juliot, near Tintagel, King Arthur's castle, on the wild Cornish coast, where he was sent to survey a ruinous church in March 1870. Amidst these romantic surroundings, Hardy met, in the person of the rector's sister-in-law, his future wife Emma Gifford.

Just before leaving for St Juliot, Hardy had submitted the manuscript of his second novel, *Desperate Remedies*, to Macmillan. On his return a month later, the 'magic' mood inspired by Emma was dispelled by Macmillan's rejecting *Desperate Remedies* as far too 'sensational' for his firm to touch. Macmillan found especially outrageous the scene of a young lady's 'violation' by her cousin. Indeed, in following Meredith's advice to make plot paramount, Hardy had, as he later admitted, relied overmuch on 'mystery, entanglement, surprise, and moral obliquity'. In effect, he had produced a 'sensation-novel', the label applied in the 1860s and 1870s to thrillers like Wilkie Collins's *The Woman in White* (1860) and Miss Braddon's *Lady Audley's Secret* (1862). However, Hardy's sensation-novel was stamped by his own themes and naive improprieties; and it deserves some attention for the light it throws on Hardy's development as a novelist as well as for its anticipations of *The Return*.

Desperate Remedies might almost have been entitled *The Poor Girl and the Lady*. A haughty chatelaine, Miss Aldclyffe, hires Cytherea Graye 'to glide round my luxurious and indolent body' as lady's maid. Indeed, in another scene that raised eyebrows at Macmillan's, Cytherea's initiation into the mysteries of the manorial toilette turns into an unconscious seduction by her mistress, who, after offering to cuff Cytherea for her awkwardness, ends by insisting that 'Cythie' share her bed. And, like Lady Audley, Miss Aldclyffe has A Secret, namely that her 'too-delicately beautiful' steward, Aeneas Manston, is actually her son, born after she had been 'cruelly betrayed' by her 'wild' cousin. Moreover, Cytherea herself turns out to be the daughter of the 'true lover' whom Miss Aldclyffe had renounced because of her ruin. Recognizing Cytherea, Miss Aldclyffe conspires to marry the girl to Manston, as if to fulfil her own love for Cytherea's dead father. Accordingly, Cytherea is separated from her own suitor, Edward Springrove, an architect and the son of a farmer, and subjected to the mesmeric presence of Manston, who is secretly married already but disposes of his wife, accidentally killing her in the process. Unaccountably frightened of Manston, Cytherea has a dream in which she is whipped, in bonds, by a masked executioner who resembles Manston. In her haplessness Cytherea, though a more living character, recalls Laura Fairlie, the victim of a similarly elaborate conspiracy in *The Woman in White*. Moreover, just as Laura is finally rescued from her criminal husband by her faithful lover, so Cytherea is rescued, after going through the wedding ceremony with Manston but before he can consummate the marriage, by Springrove.

In depicting the Aldclyffe manor, if not its mistress's arrogance, Hardy drew on Kingston Maurward. Moreover, he combined the theme of aristocratic arrogance with that of lineal decadence, a theme implicit in the 'cadaverous marble', 'the reclining figures of cross-legged knights, damp and green with age', in the Aldclyffe chantry, where Cytherea is to be sacrificed at the marriage altar to a degenerate scion. However, of more direct concern to us are the various anticipations of *The Return*. These include first of all Cytherea's dream of subjection to a masked executioner, which crudely anticipates Eustacia's sinister dream of a visored dancing partner. Secondly, the personality of the 'voluptuous' Aeneas Manston looks forward to that of the 'lady-killing' Damon Wildeve. Finally, Springrove, the farmer's son, prefigures that other farmer's son, Clym, for Springrove is the prototype in Hardy's line of men disabled as Springrove is 'through his seeing too far into things . . . thinking o' perfection in things, and then sickened that there's no such thing as perfection'.

Once it had dawned on Hardy that Macmillan was scarcely the appropriate publisher for *Desperate Remedies*, he submitted his manuscript to William Tinsley, a far less prestigious publisher, who finally agreed to publish it if Hardy would deposit £75 as a guarantee against loss. Hardy made the deposit – and deleted the offensive scene of Miss Aldclyffe's defloration – and *Desperate Remedies* appeared, anonymously, in March 1871. The early reviews, though chiding the author's 'coarseness', were on the whole not unfavourable; but then *The Spectator* effectively doomed the novel by declaring it unfit for family reading. Hardy always believed, as he wrote in his autobiography, that his damning sin had been in 'daring to suppose it possible that an unmarried lady owning an estate could have an illegitimate child'. At any rate, sales of *Desperate Remedies* fell; but though Tinsley barely recovered the costs of publishing it, he returned £60 of Hardy's deposit.

Although Hardy was already writing his third novel, *Under the Greenwood Tree*, substantial parts of which had probably been composed even before *Desperate Remedies*, the failure of *Desperate Remedies* turned his thoughts back to architecture. However, he was persuaded to 'keep a hand on the pen' by Moule as well as by Emma Gifford. Emma had even assisted Hardy by making a fair copy of the manuscript of *Desperate Remedies*; and she shared with him her intuition that his true vocation was authorship. Accordingly, Hardy finished *Under the Greenwood Tree* and sent it, in August 1871, to Macmillan. However, Macmillan, though this time finding nothing offensive in Hardy's story, seemed in no hurry to publish it. Approached some time later by Tinsley, Hardy, who had again become depressed by his prospects in literature, allowed the latter shrewd publisher to buy the copyright outright for £30. But, like many other inexperienced authors, Hardy had, to his cost, not anticipated the turning-point of his career; for when *Under the Greenwood Tree* appeared, it was a striking critical success.

Yet, despite his diffidence in dealing with publishers, Hardy had carefully designed *Under the Greenwood Tree*, his first novel set wholly in village society, to be a success. He had noted that in his first two novels the rural scenes and peasant characters had been singled out for praise. He realized also that the reading public's taste for rural or pastoral themes had recently been cultivated, notably by George Eliot in novels like *Adam Bede* (1859). It must have struck him that he was in a unique position to write an authentic pastoral novel, for Eliot, as Hardy observed in his autobiography, 'had never touched the life of the fields: her country-people having seemed to him, too, more like small townsfolk than rustics'. The true English pastoral tradition, Hardy believed, descended through Shakespeare and Fielding, but he was now well aware that the broad and earthy part of this tradition would have no place in a

Victorian pastoral. Also deliberately excluded were the sensationalism, 'socialism' and complexities of plot that had variously marked his earlier novels, though some scenes of *Under the Greenwood Tree* had been salvaged from *The Poor Man and the Lady*.

In short, in *Under the Greenwood Tree: A Rural Painting of the Dutch School* Hardy was out to create an idyll. He achieved the static perfection of that form through such effects or structures as the genre scene-painting implied by the subtitle, the humorous but authentic characterization, and the seasonal organization characteristic of pastoral tradition and suggesting timelessness. In its part-sequence – Winter, Spring, Summer, Autumn – and Conclusion (i.e. Wedding), *Under the Greenwood Tree* explicitly anticipates the implicit seasonal organization of *The Return*. However, the narrator of Hardy's Arcadia is certainly distanced from the personae, who are, after all, transformations of Hardy's own relatives and neighbours. Consequently, some critics have accused Hardy of patronizing his rustics, although this supposed condescension is probably only Hardy's attempt to assimilate the 'typical' reader's perspective. Undoubtedly, he had excluded much of his insight into rural life; he hints in his 1912 preface to the novel that he might have made quite a different story of his subject, if his public had allowed it. But he did not entirely exclude the theme of social inequality: Dick Dewy, the son of the village tranter (carrier), does defeat Farmer Shiner and Parson Maybold for the hand of Miss Fancy Day, the schoolmistress. All in all, the reviewers were delighted.

When the critical success of *Under the Greenwood Tree* was evident – though the book was not selling well – Tinsley made an offer for Hardy's work in progress, *A Pair of Blue Eyes*. But this time Hardy declined to sell his copyright. By now he understood how publishers made money. A new novel was first serialized over many months in a periodical – many publishers ran a house magazine for this purpose – and then printed in a 'three decker' or three-volume first edition, which, to be profitable, usually had to be saleable to the notoriously prudish circulating libraries. If demand warranted it, there could then be further editions; and, with the right connections, the whole procedure might be repeated in America. Hardy finally accepted Tinsley's offer of £200 for the serial and first-edition rights only of his still largely unwritten fourth novel. Accordingly, the first number of *A Pair of Blue Eyes* appeared in *Tinsleys' Magazine* in September 1872; and immediately afterwards, Hardy seems to have made his decision to abandon architecture, £200 being double what he could expect to earn in a year as an architectural assistant.

Moreover, Hardy now felt himself to be in a position to ask formally

for Emma's hand. How and when he had disentangled himself from
Tryphena Sparks is not known. Emma, however, unlike Tryphena and
Eliza Nicholls, was a lady – one of her paternal uncles even became
Archdeacon of London – and when Hardy presented himself to her
father, the indignant response seems to have been like a scene from *The
Poor Man and the Lady*. Yet, ironically, it was Emma who had thrown
herself at Hardy, though he may have partly concealed his family
background during the courtship. Exiled by her father's drunkenness to
her sister's remote home, where eligible bachelors were as rare as the
great bustard; financially dependent; and no longer young – in 1872 she
was thirty-two, only a few months younger than Hardy himself – Emma
faced the bleak future, as an old maid, of having to live always in a home
of which another woman was mistress. Thus her captivation of the
visiting architect had had a desperate purpose behind it. Despite Mr
Gifford's opposition, the engagement continued, although Hardy did
not feel financially secure enough to marry Emma until 1874, following
the great success of *Far from the Madding Crowd*.

Emma was certainly the model for Elfride Swancourt, the hectic and
sexually tantalizing heroine of *A Pair of Blue Eyes*. In this novel we have
another quasi-autobiographical plot and more transplanted material from
The Poor Man. Elfride, the daughter of a country rector but the descendant on her mother's side of the nobility, is courted first by Stephen
Smith, an architect seemingly from London, who arrives in Elfride's
remote Cornish village in order to survey a dilapidated church. But
Smith turns out to be the son of a local stonemason; consequently, he is
rejected out of hand as a suitor by Elfride's father, who had before
favoured him. After displaying a good deal of caprice, Elfride elopes to
London with Smith, only to change her mind again and return home
before her father has even discovered her overnight absence. Still secretly
pledged to Smith, Elfride next, by coincidence, attracts the attentions of
his mentor, the writer Henry Knight (whose relationship with Smith
clearly recalls that of Moule with Hardy). Elfride even saves the life of
Knight – for whom she jilts Smith – in another eyebrow-raising incident:
when Knight slides over the edge of a cliff, she fashions a lifeline from
her underclothes. (This incident was probably inspired by Hardy's
childhood book, *Paul and Virginia*, whose heroine, by refusing to strip
on a sinking ship, in effect martyrs herself to the same prudery that
plagued Hardy throughout his career.) However, Knight becomes disen-
chanted with Elfride when he learns of her abortive elopement with
Smith as well as of other indiscretions. These lapses which Elfride had
feared to confess spoil the fastidious Knight's image of her innocence,

just as Tess's confession is fatally to disillusion Angel Clare. Elfride then runs away again, this time after Knight, but she is brought home by her father. Fifteen months later, Knight and Smith, after meeting by chance and comparing notes, each decide to approach Elfride again. By coincidence they take the same train to Cornwall, unaware that, by an even greater and grimmer coincidence, Elfride is travelling with them in a satinwood coffin, en route to be interred with her noble ancestors. When they discover her death they begin to dispute about which of them she has died for, only to learn that she has died of the complications of a miscarriage, having married her distant cousin, Lord Luxellian.

Thus Hardy had finally expressed in *A Pair of Blue Eyes* what had been suppressed with *The Poor Man and the Lady* – a winsome heroine's spiteful persecution and inexorable destruction by Fate, the malignity of which is apparent in a series of ominous coincidences. Tinsley's reader had objected – as did various reviewers – to so grim an ending, but Hardy had stood firm. It may be noted that Elfride's malign destiny had been foreshadowed in her ancestry; her grandmother, the first Lady Elfride, had eloped and later died in childbirth. However, the theme of hereditary fatality is also apparent in the character of the rather ineffectual Stephen Smith, who thus, like Springrove in *Desperate Remedies*, again anticipates Clym. For Smith's constitution 'was one which, rare in the springtime of civilizations, seems to grow abundant as a nation gets older, individuality fades, and education spreads; that is, his brain had extraordinary receptive powers and no great creativeness'.

A Pair of Blue Eyes was Hardy's initiation in serial-writing, that bane of the Victorian novelist, which kept the author on a treadmill paced to a monthly deadline, made careful development of the story difficult, and prevented revision. However, Hardy had been sustained throughout his first serialization by the knowledge that greater things were to come. While *A Pair of Blue Eyes* was appearing, he had received a letter from the editor of *The Cornhill*, Leslie Stephen, who liked *Under the Greenwood Tree* and wanted Hardy to write a serial for *The Cornhill*. Elated by this prospect of promotion from *Tinsleys' Magazine* to a leading journal founded by Thackeray, Hardy replied to Stephen that once *A Pair of Blue Eyes* was finished he could offer another novel in the pastoral line of *Under the Greenwood Tree*. This new novel was to be called *Far from the Madding Crowd*; and its 'chief characters would probably be a young woman-farmer, a shepherd, and a sergeant of cavalry'.

Far from the Madding Crowd was the novel which established Hardy's reputation with both the reading public and the critics. In it Hardy was able to transcend the static idyll of *Under the Greenwood Tree*, and

33

achieve a dynamic simultaneity of the mythic and the realistic. In *Far from the Madding Crowd*, the pastoral archetypes are brought startlingly to life in the early nineteenth century; Shepherd Oak is as handy with the veterinary lancet as the Arcadian flute. At the same time, the practical objects or scenes of rural life are often transfigured by an almost numinous significance. Oak's masterful but gentle shearing of a ewe in Bathsheba's presence becomes as potently symbolic as Troy's sabre exercise, which metaphorically strips Bathsheba herself in a corresponding scene. As never before, Hardy was able to forge an organic unity of plot, character and setting, enlisting as his unifying theme that primal power of 'the Great Mother' – Nature – which is both procreative and destructive. Hardy's Arcadia is firmly rooted in this elemental world of lambing and harvest, fire and storm, wedding and funeral. Here Gabriel Oak's fidelity is tested and proven, and his union with the woman-farmer becomes naturally inevitable. However, those reviewers who saw in the novel a large debt to George Eliot's moral realism were not without a point. In Bathsheba's story we have a pattern similar to the redemption through suffering which many of Eliot's female characters undergo. Bathsheba must marry a scoundrel, suffer and humble herself before the proper union with Oak is achieved.

Among the specific anticipations of *The Return* is the espial motif, (probably suggested by the Biblical story of Bathsheba's bath), which is to recur in the actions of Eustacia and Venn. We first see Bathsheba, who is admiring herself in her looking-glass, through Oak's espial; later, in a neatly parallel scene, she gazes through Oak's cottage window and sees him at his prayers. As another foreshadowing of her chastisement, she also possesses some of Eustacia's bewitching attributes: 'Bathsheba's beauty [belonged] rather to the demonian than to the angelic school'. Troy finally accuses Bathsheba of having been Satan's tool in tempting him, as Clym is to accuse Eustacia of having bewitched him. A closer parallel is that between Troy and Wildeve, both of whom lack what in *The Return* is called the 'strong puritanic force within' (IV·vi). In his heredity, Troy, the offspring of a liaison between a French governess and an earl, looks back to Manston in *Desperate Remedies*; but Troy's 'spoliation by marriage' of Bathsheba looks forward to Wildeve's betrayal of Thomasin. Indeed, the triangle of Bathsheba, the faithful Oak and the unworthy Troy anticipates the triangle of Thomasin, Venn and Wildeve; in effect, the sub-plot of *The Return* is a transformation of the main plot of the earlier novel. However, there is no anticipation of the character of Clym. The spiritual burden of 'advanced civilization' had no place in Hardy's pastoral. Nor, in this novel, though it was written while he was absorbing the shock of Moule's suicide, did Hardy find fitting or care to risk that dwelling on cosmic malevolence which had concluded *A Pair of Blue Eyes* and which was to reappear so strikingly in *The Return*. As with *Under the Greenwood Tree*, much of Hardy's deepest feeling had to be excluded from the triumphant pastoralism of *Far from the Madding Crowd*.

Far from the Madding Crowd was a striking success, both as a serial and as a book. The reviews were approving, with the notable exception of that by the invidious Henry James, who found the sheep and Oak's two sheepdogs to be the only convincing characters in the story. As a matter of course, Stephen asked Hardy for a second serial. However, in the new novel, *The Hand of Ethelberta*, Hardy centred the story on fashionable life and London society. He had been given to understand that, as a successful novelist, he must necessarily master the comedy of manners, played out in drawing room and ballroom, which had always loomed large in the English novel. Hardy was the more eager to prove himself in this mode as the very success of *Far from the Madding Crowd* seemed to be labelling him as *merely* a pastoral novelist. 'Yet he had not the slightest intention', Hardy recalls in his autobiography, 'of writing for ever about sheepfarming, as the reading public was apparently expecting him to do.' Moreover, Hardy probably saw *Ethelberta* as an opportunity to use some of the suppressed satire of *The Poor Man and the Lady*. Unfortunately, he still lacked the sophistication to compete with Meredith and Trollope in a comedy of high-society life.

In its conception *Ethelberta* was probably influenced by Meredith's *Evan Harrington* (1861), which portrays the embarrassments of a tailor's children – one of whom is a countess by marriage – moving in upper-class circles. Similarly, Hardy's heroine is a butler's daughter who passes as a lady while keeping her place in her father's family and even employing her family as servants in her household. Another autobiographical echo is in Ethelberta's being an authoress and public 'story-teller'. Like Thackeray's Becky Sharp, Ethelberta is also an unabashed fortune-hunter, though her designs are mainly to benefit her poor relatives. When her mother-in-law cuts her off for disobedience – her first husband, the son of a baronet, having died promptly after the wedding – Ethelberta attracts an elderly viscount, the grotesque roué Lord Mountclere. Here, however, Hardy reverses the usual mésalliance plot by having Ethelberta's lower-class relatives and her rejected suitor attempt, rather farcically, to prevent the butler's daughter from marrying an unsuitable aristocrat. Christopher Julian, Ethelberta's unsuccessful lover, has some interest as another in Hardy's line of ineffectual intellectuals; but, as a whole, the characters and plot of *Ethelberta* are so contrived that it is difficult to believe that Hardy's heart remained in his 'comedy of society'. What the dour Stephen made of this 'somewhat frivolous narrative', as Hardy later described *Ethelberta*, has not been recorded. But though the reviews were not as devastating as might have been expected, Stephen did not press for a third serial; and *Ethelberta* proved to mark the end of Hardy's association with *The Cornhill*.

The Genesis of *The Return of the Native*

Just as Hardy seems to have lost interest in his comedy of manners, he also soon tired of living again in London. He seems never to have been able to write well there. Long before the first edition of *Ethelberta* appeared, the Hardys had moved out of London; first to Swanage on the Dorset coast; then to Yeovil, Somerset; and finally – and most memorably – in July 1876 to Sturminster Newton ('Stourcastle' in Wessex) in north Dorset. Here, living in Riverside Villa overlooking the Stour, their first proper household, Hardy and Emma were to experience 'the Sturminster Newton idyll ... Our happiest time'. Yet it was no literary idyll on which Hardy was now at work. Although we do not know precisely when Hardy began to work on *The Return*, the whole of its planning and composition probably took place during the nearly two years in Sturminster Newton. The Hardys returned to London in March 1878, partly in order to enable Hardy to pursue research on the Napoleonic period for his eighth novel, *The Trumpet-Major* (1880), but mainly in order to gratify Emma's desire to live again in the capital.

Thus, in its very title, *The Return of the Native* speaks of the great symbolic significance of the author's return to Dorset, following the disappointment of *Ethelberta* and probably also of London social life, in which Hardy was not comfortable. For Hardy, the 'Sturminster Newton idyll' was evidently a period of self-immersion and renewed commitment to his native vision. In *The Return* Hardy determined to risk more, both artistically and commercially, than he had ever risked before. He must have known that since the failure of *Ethelberta* his reputation was under some strain. Yet he now prepared to flout taste, propriety and convention in the calculated creation of a tragic and godless universe alien to the moralistic, social world of the typical Victorian novel. And, as never before, Hardy intended to coordinate plot, character, setting and theme in a total expression of the vision of life that had long been latent but suppressed in his work. However, in the immediate event, editorial interference, bowdlerization and the other exigencies of serialization considerably frustrated Hardy's intention. Indeed, it was not until the Uniform Edition of 1895, almost twenty years after its first publication, that the published text of *The Return* became what we now have. Moreover, in the Wessex Edition of 1912, the last overseen by him, Hardy added to Book VI a footnote stating that the 'happy ending' had been forced upon him, 'that the original conception of the story did not design a marriage between Thomasin and Venn. He was to have retained his isolated and weird character to the last, and to have disappeared mysteriously from the heath, nobody knowing whither – Thomasin remaining a widow.'

Hardy probably began writing *The Return* late in 1876. By February 1877 he had sent a draft of the first part of the novel to Stephen, whose caution was immediately aroused. Although he liked the opening – presumably the description of Egdon Heath – Stephen, who had ruthlessly bowdlerized *Far from the Madding Crowd*, 'feared that the relations between Eustacia, Wildeve, and Thomasin might develop into something "dangerous" for a family magazine, and he refused to have anything to do with it unless he could see the whole'. Hardy had no better luck with *Blackwood's Magazine* and *Temple Bar*; and he was finally obliged to accept an offer from the less prestigious *Belgravia*, edited by Miss Braddon, the sensation-novelist. Serialization in *Belgravia* began in January 1878, by which time Hardy had conceded the expediency of Thomasin's marriage to Venn, since he refers to their ultimate union in a letter, dated 8 February, to his illustrator. Hardy had not expected much profit from *The Return*; in fact, he received £240 for the serial, together with £200 for the three-volume first edition. These payments were a substantial reduction from the £700 he had received for the English publication of *Ethelberta*, though he was to receive some further income from the simultaneous serialization of *The Return* in America.

The Ur-Novel

In addition to what information can be gleaned from the publication history of *The Return*, the survival of Hardy's original manuscript, bearing many interlineal revisions, has permitted important insights into the genesis of the novel. From this manuscript textual critics, notably John Paterson, have been able partially to reconstruct a putative 'Ur-version' of *The Return*. Hardy's revisions from this Ur-version, apart from some bowdlerization, consistently show an edification of both character and plot, in keeping with the sublimity of the opening evocation of Egdon Heath, which evidently remained unchanged as the touchstone of Hardy's intention. Perhaps the most striking revelation of the Ur-version is that Hardy seems originally to have conceived his drama of malign fate in the Gothic or fantastic mode; that is, in the Ur-version supernatural malevolence is literal rather than metaphoric. The prototype of Eustacia is neither a proud girl stifled by provinciality nor a Promethean rebel, but an actual witch named Avice Vye, who was apparently to have bewitched Thomasin while professing friendship. The 'blood-coloured' reddleman was also originally conceived as a 'Mephistophelian visitant' in a more literal sense (*Diggory* is a dialectal euphemism for the devil). Indeed, Hardy had already made fictional use of witchcraft and the evil eye. In *Under the Greenwood Tree*, for example, Fancy consults the village witch; more sombrely, in *A Pair of Blue Eyes* the Widow Jethway 'ill-wishes' Elfride.

However, the Gothic genesis of *The Return* was, almost certainly, also influenced by a hitherto undetected source, W. H. Ainsworth's historical romance, *The Lancashire Witches* (1848). Hardy was an avid reader of Ainsworth from boyhood, and the parallels between *Lancashire Witches* and *The Return* are striking. In particular, Avice's persecution of the Ur-Thomasin is prefigured in Ainsworth's plot, in which Alizon Device, dark and flowing-haired, is suspected of bewitching a fair girl, her beloved's sister, just as the Ur-Thomasin is Clym's sister. Moreover, the name 'Alizon Device' is echoed in 'Avice', a name which Hardy found, like 'Eustacia' (originally 'Eustachia'), in local annals. In addition, the following suggestive features of Ainsworth's story may be listed: (1) an opening, infernally depicted bonfire scene in November on a hill dominating a 'heathy waste', the central fire being answered by other fires at points roundabout; (2) the appearance at the central fire of an 'unearthly' figure, who has an uncanny knowledge of the heath and later dresses in 'blood-red' garb; (3) the embodiment of the desolation by a woman outlined against the sky atop a cairn; (4) a character's 'filial regard' for his native hills in contradistinction to an outsider's disdain; (5) the general use of dialect and local folklore, including Maypole-dancing and mumming; (6) the particular use of witchcraft, including image magic, witch-pricking, the hourglass and the lunar eclipse; (7) the portrayal of the witch as both diabolical enemy and sacrificial victim; (8) the use of a heath-pool as a trysting place and the agitation of its water as a signal; (9) a demonic tempter with a courtly mode of discourse like Damon Wildeve's; (10) the depiction of characters as puppets of 'Fatality'; (11) the 'triumph' of 'Fate' in the destruction of Alizon and her lover; and (12) the final display of the dead lovers, 'pale and beautiful . . . as sculptured marble'.

But these parallels are listed not to show that Hardy lacked originality, but rather to suggest that the Ur-version enables us to glimpse Hardy in the process of transforming Ainsworth's local colour and vulgar supernaturalism into thematic structures of infinitely greater power. First of all, the wild landscape and rustic life which Ainsworth exploited for their picturesqueness, quaintness or humour, as it served his turn, become organic in Hardy's evolving work; the Egdon Heath overture establishes both wild nature and folk nature as aspects of an enduring, universal pattern. Next we have the transference of eternal malignity from Satan and his human agents to a cosmic 'coil of things' (II:vi) or impersonal Necessity. The witch Avice thus becomes the Promethean Eustacia; but in the absence of a divine tyrant, Eustacia's rebellion against the conditions of existence can end only in ironic self-destruction. In *The Lancashire Witches* the hourglass is associated with the traditional Faustian 'bargain'; and as the sands run out 'like a current of life blood', Ainsworth's passionate and beautiful witch seizes the glass, 'as if she could arrest her destiny by the act'. However, Eustacia's hourglass (the manuscript shows her telescope was an afterthought) is the symbol of a private 'bad bargain with life' (V:iv); the 'peculiar pleasure [Eustacia] derived from watching a material representation of time's gradual glide away' (I:vii) is the symptom of a personal, existential alienation. At the same time, Eustacia remains a witch for the heath-folk; and the witch persona persists under the surface of her characterization. Hence, in the Ur-version, we can see Hardy evolving his multiple-level mode of presentation, his ability to create a narrative simultaneity of the literal or realistic and the metaphoric or mythic.

Another striking feature of the Ur-version of *The Return* is the low social status and narrow horizons of the characters. Originally, they are all natives of the same heath; and even the Yeobrights speak in dialect. Venn is first identified as the grandson of Grandfer Cantle rather than as the son of a prosperous dairyman. Mrs Yeobright is nothing so genteel as a curate's daughter, and Clym himself, as a mere 'jeweller's assistant' in Budworth, is not given the honorific, Mr, by the heath-folk. Paris is not mentioned. But Hardy's evolving Wessex setting soon required an outside perspective for its realization. Consequently, as Avice–Eustacia's role developed from witch or temptress to tragic protagonist – and as Thomasin's role correspondingly diminished – Paris was introduced as an antipodal contrast to Egdon. This extension of horizon, in turn, facilitated the double view of the heath as repellent and alien (from the perspective of Eustacia and Wildeve), but at the same time maternal and sublime (from the Yeobrights' perspective). This dual perspective was to be sharpened by the main characters' elevation in status and education; moreover, such an elevation proved necessary for the tragic perspective which Hardy was developing. If Paris was the antipodes of Wessex, Attica was ultimately to be recognized as its prototype; and Clym was to need every advantage of dignity and learning to support the weight of Oedipus and Orestes that came to rest upon him.

One additional feature of the Ur-version may be noted here: a freedom of expression and candour which were to require censorship later. On the trivial level, this was to mean the expurgation of mild oaths such as 'Oh God!' More serious were certain apparently slighting references to Christianity or the deity which had to be deleted or modified in the first edition. For example, in the manuscript and serial version, Eustacia bitterly notes 'the cruel satires that *God* loves to indulge in' (III:v); but *God* becomes *Fate* in the first edition. Similarly, the clause, 'Christianity was eclipsed in their hearts', applied to Eustacia and Wildeve in the 'gipsying' scene (IV:iii), was deleted in the first edition. Bowdlerization also marked Hardy's revision for publication. In the Ur-version, Wildeve, who is originally an older and more hardened sinner, ironically named Toogood, apparently tricks Thomasin by an invalid marriage ceremony and lives with her for a week before she discovers the deception and returns to Blooms-End. Such a cruel betrayal more naturally explains Thomasin's distress than the simple postponement of the wedding as a result of Wildeve's failing to secure the correct licence. Obviously, Hardy's editor thought Thomasin's original predicament too shocking. Moreover, Hardy had compounded his indiscretion by originally entitling the chapter (II:viii) describing Thomasin's eventual marriage to the unloving Wildeve 'Happiness Must Needs Be Sacrificed to Propriety', a title so unacceptably challenging to Mrs Grundy that it too was suppressed.

Published Versions of *The Return of the Native*

Let us now look briefly at the development of *The Return* through its various published versions. In its first appearance in print, as the serial in *Belgravia*, *The Return* was markedly different – in style, detail and theme – from the novel we now read. Stylistically, for example, the text reflects its magazine context, abounding in what Moule called 'Tinsleyan' style, i.e. verbosity, exclamation and genteelism (such as 'female' for 'woman'). Significant details of plot are underdeveloped. Clym is still a mere jeweller's assistant; and Eustacia, as the daughter of a *Belgian* bandmaster, lacks her suggestive Hellenic ancestry. Moreover, the relations between Eustacia and Wildeve are unclear, and Hardy's treatment of the dangerous subject of adultery evasive. Thus the fatal quarrel between Mrs Yeobright and Eustacia is precipitated not by the former's apparent insinuation about a gift from Wildeve, but simply by her restatement of opposition to her son's marriage. Similarly, in Book V,

Eustacia and Wildeve have no intention of eloping; and Eustacia's suicide is attributed solely to her unwillingness to accept Wildeve's offer of money for her flight.

Hardy extensively revised this serial text – and added his map of the scene of the novel – for the three-volume first edition published by Smith, Elder. In this second major published version of *The Return*, Hardy eliminated much of the stylistic preciosity that had characterized the serial text, and generally made the language more direct and forceful (though the euphemism 'illness' for 'pregnancy' survives all of Hardy's revisions). For example, the turf-cutter's remark, in the serial version, that Thomasin 'must be a fool to tear her cap' (I:iii) for Wildeve becomes, more authentically, 'tear her *smock*'. On the other hand, Hardy deleted – and never restored – the 'anti-Christian' passages already mentioned which had somehow escaped the serial editor's censorship. The process of the main characters' social edification also continues in the first edition, Clym being promoted to 'jeweller's manager' and given a curate as a maternal grandfather. Most significantly, plot and characterization are improved by making the relationship between Eustacia and Wildeve more clearly passionate and by making Wildeve's supposed gift of the guineas won from Christian the immediate cause of the quarrel between Mrs Yeobright and Eustacia. Yet, in an edition intended to sell to the circulating libraries, Hardy was still unable to deal explicitly with the motive of adultery; in the scenes between Eustacia and Wildeve following their respective marriages, Wildeve preserves an uncharacteristic respect for the marriage vow. As in the serial text, no mention is made of their eloping together; and Eustacia still apparently drowns herself because she is too proud to accept his money.

The reviews of the first edition of *The Return* justified the fears that had led to its bowdlerization. Though noting that Eustacia and Wildeve 'know no other law than the gratification of their own passion', the reviewer in *The Athenaeum*, seeing that the proprieties had been sufficiently observed, passed *The Return* as fit to be read in 'respectable households'. However, he detected that Eustacia 'belongs essentially to the class of which [Flaubert's] Madame Bovary is the type'; and he rather smugly chided Hardy for having 'wasted his powers' in the partial and misleading portrait of a character which 'English opinion' will 'not allow a novelist to depict in its completeness'. Not that the portrayal of adulterous passion, even in a wife, was absolutely taboo in popular fiction. In *David Copperfield* (1850) and *Hard Times* (1854), for example, Dickens had shown the maudlin repentance of young wives – married to much older husbands – who are so tempted. In *Dombey and Son* (1848), Dickens asks us to believe that Mrs Dombey elopes to France with

Carker, with no thought of allowing him to become her lover. Hardy, on the other hand, refusing either to abandon his subject or to resort to sentimentalization and hypocrisy, produced, for the time being, the incompleteness noted by the *Athenaeum* reviewer.

The reviewers found various other lapses of propriety as well as a general lack of realism. The *Athenaeum* reviewer was puzzled by the 'low social position of the characters'; on the other hand, the reviewers objected that Hardy's rustics spoke not like Hodge in *Punch*, but too fluently and poetically. *The Saturday Review* remarked that Wessex apparently lacked market-towns, highroads and stagecoaches; and 'we hear nothing of a squire'. Of course, *The Return* was also faulted for its unfashionable sombreness and lack of sentiment. Writing in *The Academy*, W. E. Henley, the chauvinistic poet, found the portrayal of unhappiness in the novel 'very cruel, and very French'. Henley also complained that the author 'rarely makes you laugh and never makes you cry'; 'rare artist as [Hardy] is,' Henley concluded, 'there is something wanting in his personality, and he is not quite a great man.' Though usually accompanied by acknowledgements of Hardy's genius and power, the reviewers' general hesitancy was reflected in the poor sales of *The Return*.

Hardy was not to have another opportunity to revise *The Return* until 1895, when the first collected edition of his fiction was published. However, this Uniform Edition of *The Return* was more than a revision, more than a delayed response to the reviewers. It was, in effect, a reconstruction of the novel which bowdlerization had nearly ruined in the first edition of 1878. Hardy had evidently been biding his time. There are few parallels in literary history of a major novel's going through such textual vicissitudes before achieving such a long-delayed restoration. In 1895, too, Hardy had just completed what was to prove to be his last novel, *Jude the Obscure*, which was greeted with vilification of its author; and we might well ask whether the history of *The Return*, now so fresh in Hardy's mind, influenced his decision to abandon novel-writing.

However that may be, in this third published version of *The Return*, Hardy, in the first place, rationalized his Wessex geography, suppressing his map of Egdon and, now apparently seeing no reason to conceal the Stinsford original of his setting, substituting 'Rainbarrow' for 'Blackbarrow'. He also called attention to the Shakespearean implication of his setting by identifying Egdon Heath with 'the heath of that traditionary King of Wessex – Lear.' Perhaps partly as a response to the reviewers' objections to his characters' low social status, but more likely to suit his own developed conception of tragic dignity, Hardy now heightened Mrs Yeobright's social ambition and raised Clym to manager in a diamond merchant's establishment. Moreover, Eustacia's queenly airs were now made more credible by the revelation of her matrilineal descent from the English nobility; and the transformation of her father from a Belgian into an Ionian 'Ulysses' allowed another thematic symmetry, in the patrilineal descent of the naturally pagan Eustacia from ancient Greece. The implicit identification of Wessex with Attica as well as the implicit Oedipal theme was also now confirmed by an equation of Clym's horror, on his discovery of his wife's role in his mother's death, with 'studies of Oedipus' (V:ii). In addition to this tightening and enrichment of thematic structure, Hardy again thoroughly revised the text for style, cutting much of the verbal inflation that still survived from the serial version, particularly the vestiges of stage-villain rhetoric in Wildeve's speeches. The result was a restrained diction accordant with the sombre dignity of the Egdon Heath overture.

Finally, in this remarkable 1895 revision Hardy was at last able to be frank concerning the sexual attraction between Eustacia and Wildeve and their final plan to run away together to Paris. For example, he added a significant clause (italicized here) to Eustacia's reproaches of Wildeve during their first bonfire tryst: 'I have had no word with you since you – you chose [Thomasin], and walked about with her, and deserted me entirely, *as if I had never been yours body and soul so irretrievably!*' (I:vi). Furthermore, Eustacia's final despair on Rainbarrow is now clearly attributed to her recognition of the moral pettiness of the man whose mistress she is about to become: 'He's not *great* enough for me to give myself to – he does not suffice for my desire! ... If he had been a Saul or a Bonaparte – ah! But to break my marriage vow for him – it is too poor a luxury!' (V:vii). As she is finally presented, Eustacia is as convincing a victim of pride as her supposed 'type', Emma Bovary, had been a victim of romantic illusion.

When Macmillan published the definitive Wessex Edition in 1912, Hardy took advantage of the opportunity to make one final revision of *The Return*. This last version, which is the usual copy-text for modern editions, introduces fewer changes than any of Hardy's other revisions. In addition to various small adjustments in diction tending to make the dialogue slightly less dialectal than in the 1895 edition, we may note that Hardy reintroduced a certain ambiguity in the relations between Eustacia and Wildeve by altering Eustacia's reproach already quoted. In the 1912 text she chides Wildeve for deserting her, 'as if I had never been yours *life* and soul so irretrievably!' Hardy also added the sentence, 'Even the receipt of Clym's letter would not have stopped her now' (V:vii), to the comment on Eustacia's desperate preparations for the flight that is to end in catastrophe while this same letter of reconciliation is ironically delayed. This addition, it has been argued, weakens the sense of fatal circumstance and coincidence which Hardy has been at such pains to build up; on the other hand, the interpolated sentence might be taken as a reminder that the forces driving Eustacia inevitably to her death derive as much from innate character as from external coincidence. Oddly enough, Hardy still did not correct at least one notable inconsistency surviving from the first edition: in Chapter 11 of Book I Mrs Yeobright refuses to tell Wildeve the name of Thomasin's other suitor; but in Chapter 7 of Book II we hear that she did name Venn to Wildeve, who, in turn, tells Eustacia.

As already mentioned, the Wessex Edition of *The Return* is also distinguished by Hardy's footnote intimating, now that the last revision has been made, that the published novel still falls short of the ideal novel of the author's original conception thirty-five years before; that most of Book VI, including Venn's Maypole courtship of Thomasin, is inconsistent with the requirements of 'an austere artistic code'. We shall postpone our discussion of the problems in unity raised by Book VI; but we may note here that, presumably, Hardy's ideal novel (originally in five books to match the traditional five acts of tragedy) was to have ended with a funeral, not a wedding; perhaps, too, there was to have been a chapter of elegiac epilogue to match the Egdon Heath prologue. In any event, it is unlikely that Hardy could have sold Smith, Elder or any other prominent publisher a novel with such austerity of form – and with no reassuring 'Aftercourses' – in 1878. It is interesting to note, however, that in that same year Hardy did publish a story stark and nihilistic in its catastrophe. This was his novelette *An Indiscretion in the Life of an Heiress*, which incorporates much of the plot of *The Poor Man and the Lady*, including the last-minute striking down of the heroine, and which perhaps reflects something of the austerity of the lost ending of *The Return*.

Autobiographical Implications in *The Return of the Native*

We come now, in conclusion of this section, to our postponed discussion of the autobiographical implications of *The Return*. By 1912, when the Wessex Edition appeared, many of Hardy's readers were aware of the topographical correspondences between Egdon and Stinsford, correspondences which Hardy himself to some extent clarified, for the convenience of 'searchers for scenery', in his prefatory remarks to the 1895 and 1912 editions. However, he was not so ready to acknowledge correspondence in human character. While making his last revision of *The Return*, Hardy recorded: 'I got to like the character of Clym before I had done with him. I think he is the nicest of all my heroes, and *not a bit like me*'. But despite this slightly disingenuous disavowal, biographical criticism has focused on the correspondence between Clym and his creator; and here we too shall begin.

In the first place, Hardy gave Clym the Christian name of his own supposed ancestor, Clement le Hardy. Clym's surname is presumably derived from the river Yeo in Somerset, which flows through Yeovil where Hardy lived just before beginning *The Return*. However, 'Yeobright' also suggests 'yeoman', the traditional class to which both Hardy and Clym – as the sons, respectively, of an artisan and a farmer – originally belonged. Hardy may have adopted the unusual diminutive 'Clym' (instead of 'Clem') after 'the good ye[o]man Clym', in the ballad 'Adam Bell, Clym of the Clough [cliff], and William of Cloudesley', which appears in one of Hardy's favourite books, Percy's *Reliques of English Poetry* (1765). Like Clym Yeobright, Clym of the Clough finally rises from yeoman to gentleman. Intriguingly, Percy's *Reliques* includes two other details related to Clym's role in *The Return*, namely the Elizabethan lyric 'My Mind to Me a Kingdom Is', which becomes the title of the chapter introducing Clym, and 'Queen Eleanor's Confession', the ballad, sung by Grandfer Cantle, relating Henry II's discovery of his consort's guilt of adultery and murder. But whether or not Hardy did derive his diminutive from 'Clym of the Clough', the choice of 'Clym Yeobright' was a considered one; in the Ur-version the native is named Hugh Britton.

The name 'Yeobright' is suggestive in another way of a parallel between Clym and Hardy. Etymologically, 'yeoman' means 'young man'; the analogous sense of 'Yeobright', 'young-bright', therefore applies to Clym and Hardy, both of whom were child prodigies. Like Hardy, Clym, known for his precocity, 'had been a lad of whom something was expected' (III:i). Another obvious parallel between the two is nostalgia for the heath, and it is almost certainly an autobiographical reflection that 'Clym had been so interwoven with the heath in his boyhood that hardly anybody could look upon it without thinking of him' (III:i). Hardy also endowed Clym with his own musical ancestry; the anecdotes recalled by the heath-folk of the prodigies of blowing and bowing performed in local church choirs by Clym's uncle are drawn from the similar exploits of Hardy's grandfather. Hardy may even have given Clym his own sister. In the Ur-version, Thomasin is Clym's sister rather than his paternal first cousin – in fact, textual traces of this original relationship persisted until the 1895 revision – and Mrs Yeobright's tone of feeling for the girl remains maternal. Hardy's biographer, Michael Millgate, suggests that the elder of Hardy's two sisters, the self-effacing Mary Hardy to whom he was especially close, was the model for Thomasin, whose unusual Christian name feminizes Hardy's common one.

But, of course, such similarities of name, ancestry and affinity point to profounder autobiographical correspondences. Here the analogue of a physical and spiritual 'return' to native grounds is central. Thus, in Clym's giving up of worldly advancement in order to become a heath schoolmaster and ultimately a preacher, we may recognize a magnification of Hardy's abandonment of architecture in favour not of his long cherished ambition of the Church, but of the teaching and preaching implicit in authorship. As we know, Hardy attributed his own lack of worldly ambition to his being the scion of 'an old family of spent social energies'; and this lineal weariness is refined to asceticism, altruism and ethereality in Clym, Clym's surname taking on here another ironic resonance. It is also, presumably, through a certain degree of authorial self-projection that Clym becomes, at the same time, the type of the 'modern' intellectual, his introspection prefiguring that of a whole, post-heroic race. In his spiritually wearied face 'could be dimly seen the typical countenance of the future' (III:i).

More clearly autobiographical is the opposition with which Clym's return is met by his widowed mother, who seems to echo Jemima Hardy's driving ambition for her children to 'get on' and 'do well': 'After all the trouble that has been taken to give you a start, and when you have nothing to do but to keep straight on towards affluence, you say you will be a poor man's schoolmaster. Your fancies will be your ruin, Clym' (III:ii). The lack of ambition supposedly shown by Hardy's own father is also echoed in Mrs Yeobright's reproaches of her son: 'I suppose you will be like your father; like him, you are weary of doing well' (III:ii). The autobiographical implications here are confirmed by Jemima's opposition to Hardy's abandonment of his architectural career and by her persistent scepticism regarding writing as a profession. Hardy later admitted that the vehement but maternally devoted Mrs Yeobright was, indeed, a finished portrait of his own mother, just as Mrs Dewy in *Under the Greenwood Tree* and Mrs Smith in *A Pair of Blue Eyes*, with their yeoman-class pride, had been earlier studies of Jemima.

Certainly another trait derived from Jemima is the passionate devotion to Clym and Thomasin which underlies Mrs Yeobright's gruffness and coldness. The very closeness of Clym and his mother – their discourses being 'as if carried on between the right and left hands of the same body'

(III:iii) – is what makes their conflict so ominous. Hardy's biographers generally agree on the existence of a similarly powerful, if undemonstrative, bond between Hardy and his mother, a bond apparently not approached in emotional strength by either of his marriages. It is also generally accepted that the powerful influence exerted by Jemima, if it stimulated Hardy's development of genius, was ultimately distorting in effect. As if himself testifying to the immaturity resulting from his mother's domination, Hardy recorded: 'I was a child till I was 16; a youth till I was 25; a young man till I was 40 or 50.'

Furthermore, Mrs Yeobright's bitter jealousy of Eustacia is probably modelled on the hostility to poor Emma Hardy displayed by Jemima, who seems to have thought her son's wife unworthy of him and who was opposed to his marrying at all. Apparently, one reason that Hardy, in the years immediately following his marriage to Emma, lived in Yeovil, Sturminster Newton, or anywhere but Dorchester, was to keep the two women apart. Indeed, Hardy was not to settle in the Dorchester area until 1883, although Jemima lived until 1904, predeceasing Emma by only eight years.

Another of Hardy's biographers, Robert Gittings, has seen additional evidence of an Oedipus complex in Hardy's sexual predilection for his maternal first cousins, the Sparks sisters, who resembled Jemima both physically and emotionally. Thus Clym's suppressed sexual interest in Thomasin is another parallel with his creator, though of course in the final version of the story she is not a relation by blood of Mrs Yeobright. It must also be kept in mind that romance between cousins is so common in Victorian fiction as to be usually unremarkable. But if we are looking for an incest pattern in *The Return*, it is surely suggestive that Clym's boyhood playmate should have been transformed from sister in the Ur-version to marriageable cousin in the novel. It is also suggestive that Mrs Yeobright should desire the union of these two virtual siblings. Such unconsciously incestuous overtones seem to be inseparable from the emotion of Clym's return to the scenes of his childhood and, above all, to the maternal household. We may certainly see in *The Return* an adumbration of the relationship of Paul Morel and his fiercely possessive mother in Lawrence's *Sons and Lovers* (1913).

The correspondent maternal jealousy of Mrs Yeobright and Jemima also suggests, as intimated by Michael Millgate, at least a symbolic identification of Eustacia with Emma. As we know, Emma had already served as the model for Elfride, the doomed heroine of *A Pair of Blue Eyes*, who is disparaged as a prospective daughter-in-law by Mrs Smith, the prototype of Mrs Yeobright. Elfride, it will be recalled, is also 'ill-wished' by the uncanny Widow Jethway, who in her hatred of the heroine for supposedly harming her son anticipates Susan Nunsuch. We have, then, in both *A Pair of Blue Eyes* and *The Return* (though to a less developed degree in the former) a pattern in which maternal hostility to the heroine is dissociated, its irrational component being projected onto a witch-mother who becomes a Gothic shadow of the respectable mother. Apart from being a victim of maternal jealousy, however, the rebellious and challenging Eustacia, fittingly surnamed 'Vye', seems at first glance to have little in common with the devout Emma, who always felt that 'an Unseen Power of great benevolence directs my ways'. Still, Clym's discovery of a beautiful, passionate and unconventional young lady dwelling incongruously on a remote heath does recall Hardy's own meeting with the susceptible Emma in the lonely Cornish rectory, where circumstances made her seem more romantic and unconventional than she actually was. Similarly, Eustacia's predisposition to fall in love with Clym, the glamorous stranger from Paris who seems to offer escape from the heath, recalls the girlish anxiety of the thirty-year-old Emma in anticipation of the visit of the London architect, on whom she had already based matrimonial hopes. To some extent, too, the conjugal incompatibility of Clym and Eustacia doubtless reflects Hardy's growing disillusionment with Emma, which was to culminate in virtual estrangement during the latter years of their marriage. Eustacia's urging of Clym to take her to Paris, at least, may well echo Emma's pressure on Hardy, while he was writing *The Return* in Sturminster Newton, to take her back to London.

Probably the central autobiographical significance of *The Return* is expressed in Millgate's suggestion that the novel may be read as a private cautionary tale in which Hardy was warning himself of the personal catastrophe in store if he should yield to the seductive pull of nostalgia and attempt to 'return' other than imaginatively. In effect, Clym's misjudgements demonstrate Hardy's growing realization that idealism and intellectuality could not be transplanted in the provinces; that in many respects the worlds of London and Higher Bockhampton were irreconcilable; that Emma and Jemima would never willingly share his love; and that, as the youthful prodigy from the heath who had become part of the great world outside, he could never return home. Thus Clym, that personality of great promise and great failure, who is torn by a fatal self-conflict externalized in the conflict with his mother, is his creator's monitory alter ego, drawn from Hardy's deepest self-knowledge. The common criticisms that Hardy's fascination with Clym is obtrusive and that Clym's twin roles of tragic protagonist and didactic philanthropist are discrepant must take into account the acuteness of irony and re-markable self-detachment with which Clym's deterioration is presented; it is a fine stroke to make him literally as well as metaphorically blind. Similarly, a supreme psychological insight is apparent in the dream-like evening scene in which Clym, after hearing without recognition her cry, suddenly finds himself bending over his dying mother: momentarily, 'all sense of time and place left him, and it seemed as if he and his mother were as when he was a child with her many years ago on this heath at hours similar to the present' (IV:vii). With its ironic recall of Words-worth's 'Intimations of Immortality from Recollections of Early Childhood' (1807), this epiphany on the maternal heath typifies the tragic nostalgia inherent not only in the return of Hardy's native, but in a whole post-Romantic convention of lost innocence and hopeless longing. In short, in Clym we can see Hardy transforming a personal crisis into a universal theme.

2. *The Return of the Native* and Victorian Thought

In this chapter we place *The Return* in the context of cultural and intellectual history. In its first edition in 1878, certain ideological features were already apparent: these included the portrayal of an instinctive 'paganism' in the characters, together with a notable absence of Christianity; the implication, through malign coincidence and hostile environment, of a cosmic order indifferent to, or even favouring, human suffering; the implication, through class bias and marital mismatches, of a social order complementing the cosmic order in its hostility to human happiness; and, in general, the sense of a fatality overruling character, aspiration and morality. The reviewers tended to attribute these discomfiting features to foreign influences such as the pessimism of Schopenhauer and the naturalism of Flaubert, whose notorious *Madame Bovary* had appeared in 1857. But though Hardy may have been influenced by Flaubert's ironic study of adultery, he does not seem to have known Schopenhauer while writing *The Return*; in any case, not reading German, Hardy could not have studied Schopenhauer's main work, *The World as Will and Representation* (1819), until after its translation into English in 1883. It is in Hardy's later works, especially in the portrayal of the 'Immanent Will' in his epic-drama *The Dynasts* (1904–8), that some parallel with Schopenhauer's philosophy may be found. We shall begin our background of *The Return* nearer home.

Hardy's loss of faith in Christianity during his London years in the 1860s was gradual; unlike many of his contemporaries, he does not seem to have undergone a crisis of doubt. His personal brand of agnosticism – the word 'agnostic' was coined by T. H. Huxley in 1870 – appears to have been largely a natural development from the scepticism bred by his self-education; and the folk fatalism of his native background is a more immediate source than Schopenhauer for the doubt of cosmic benevolence implicit in *The Return*. But though Hardy was never as intellectually sophisticated as, say, George Eliot, who was even capable of translating the latest German work of sceptical scholarship, he was extraordinarily sensitive to the intellectual currents of his time; and most of these, including Positivism, Darwinism and the higher criticism, left their mark upon him. In 1875 Hardy was called upon to witness Leslie Stephen's symbolic declaration of agnosticism, his signature on a document renouncing holy orders; and the two men then discussed the obsolescence of theology.

The Climate of Doubt

Let us now look in more detail at the history of the ideas behind that crisis in religious faith which frames *The Return*. The rise of doubt, first in the literal truth of the Bible and finally in the very existence of God, could be traced back to the Renaissance. However, its more immediate source was eighteenth-century rationalism, as exemplified by David Hume and Voltaire, for the recent intellectual triumphs of the physical sciences had established the independence of human reason from divine inspiration. Thus, when Napoleon publicly challenged La Place on the absence of God from his cosmology, the physicist made his famous denial of any need for 'that hypothesis'. During the early Victorian period the autonomy of science was most influentially expounded by another Frenchman, Auguste Comte, the founder of Positivism. He taught that man's intellectual activity, both in the race and the individual, has developed in three 'states' or stages, the first or *theological* stage being that of belief in spirits, myths and gods; the second or *metaphysical* stage being that of abstract philosophy, with its futile speculation on final causes and essences of being; and the final or *positive* stage being that presently reached in Western Europe, in which man rightly focuses on material reality and the classification of facts. With its echoes of Utilitarianism, Positivism seemed to express the very ethos of the age of Darwin and J. S. Mill; and Stephen was probably recalling Comte's theory of the three stages when he told Hardy, after signing his renunciation of holy orders, 'that he had "wasted" much time on systems of religion and metaphysics'.

Moreover, the Positivistic spirit, in the form of the so-called 'higher criticism' inaugurated by German philologists, had even invaded Biblical studies. This became sensationally apparent in 1860 with the publication of *Essays and Reviews*, the authors of which were seven liberal churchmen. Despite its innocuous title, this volume scandalized the pious by applying to the Holy Scriptures the same objective analysis applied to texts like the *Iliad* or *Beowulf*. By detecting textual or historical inconsistencies and mythological intrusions in the Bible, the higher critics tended to cast doubt on the whole miraculous element in Christian history. Already, in 1843, George Eliot had translated a German biography of Jesus which seemed to relegate its subject to the realm of mythology.

However, in keeping with an era of Positivism, the decisive blow against orthodoxy in religious belief was struck by science. In the early nineteenth century the new discipline of geology was already in conflict with the quasi-Biblical dogma that God had created the world on 23 October 4004 B C – not to speak of the scientific indefensibility of Noah's flood or Moses's rolling back the Red Sea. Geological investigation not only demonstrated that the earth is infinitely older than allowed for in the chronology of Genesis, but also produced startling fossil evidence of successive worlds of extinct animals and plants unknown to Adam. In fact, biology soon succeeded geology as the major subversive influence. As geology had challenged Biblical chronology, biology was soon challenging the dogma of the fixity of natural species, a dogma which had become central to Christian apology, because only such fixity seemed consistent with God's instantaneous creation of life. Even before Darwin, the accumulating evidence of fossils, comparative anatomy and embryology had driven biologists to the conclusion that species have mutated and evolved through a process requiring the aeons of time recorded in the geological record.

Thus the stage was set for the epoch-making appearance of Darwin's *On the Origin of Species* (1859), which not only presented the evidence of evolution, but also provided a convincing explanation of the mechanism, namely natural selection, by which evolution occurs. Disliking controversy, Darwin had reserved his discussion of man in *On the Origin of Species*; but he finally set out his proofs of man's simian ancestry in *The Descent of Man* (1871). In response to his critics' mockery, Darwin allowed himself one dry witticism in *The Descent*: those who sneer at evolution, he observed, simultaneously expose evidence of it in their canine teeth. The devastating impact of the theory of evolution upon the traditional Christian world-view can be better understood if we remember that Darwin and his followers, perhaps inspired by Comte's theory of the successive stages of man's intellectual development, applied the evolutionary principle to man's mental as well as physical development: anticipating Freud, Darwin inferred that social feeling, morality, and even religion itself, had all originated in animal instincts. Accordingly he was forced to take issue with the theological position that the so-called savage races of mankind represent a sinful degeneration from the original perfection of Eden; and his identification of savagery as an ancestral stage of civilization became the basis of the new science of anthropology.

The Pains of Agnosticism

Still, however well-founded the intellectual bases of Victorian agnosticism were, the experience of apostasy was often traumatic. For if it was the age of Comte and Darwin, it was still the age of Muscular Christianity. As Hardy recalls in his autobiography, the seven authors of *Essays and Reviews* were pilloried in the press as 'the Seven against Christ'; and one of them, Benjamin Jowett, was nearly deprived of his tutorship at Oxford. In 1864 11,000 British clergymen signed an indignant reconfirmation of the divine inspiration of the Bible and of the existence of Hell. Indeed, it was this violent emotional reaction to doubt which obliged Hardy to adopt indirectness of expression in referring to the deity in *The Return*. Even nearly twenty years after the publication of *The Return*, however, *Jude the Obscure* was burned – privately – by an Anglican bishop, Hardy remarking in a later preface to *Jude* that the bishop had burned the book 'probably in his despair at not being able to burn me'.

Yet the trauma of agnosticism was probably due as much to inner conflict as to external antagonism. The emotional opposition to agnosticism was also within the agnostic himself, perhaps in the form of nostalgia for an innocence lost with the old faith, perhaps as a recognition that agnosticism had not abolished man's need for a God or given man the strength to bear life in a Godless universe. Thus the narrator in *Tess* speaks of 'the chronic melancholy which is taking hold of the civilized races with the decline of belief in a beneficent Power'. This fatal division between intellect and feeling was a significant aspect of that universal split personality often seen as characteristic of the Victorian period. Hardy himself rather irrationally complains in his autobiography that his intellectual posture had obscured his emotional Anglicanism,

that although invidious critics had cast slurs upon him as Nonconformist, Agnostic, Atheist, Infidel, Immoralist, Heretic, Pessimist . . . they never thought of calling him what they might have called him much more plausibly – churchy; not in an intellectual sense, but in so far as instincts and emotions ruled.

The pains of agnosticism also reflected the apprehension of what that most influential of Victorian sages, Carlyle, in his tract *Chartism* (1839), called the 'blind No-God, of Necessity and Mechanism, that held men like a hideous World-Steam engine, like a hideous Phalaris' Bull, imprisoned in its own iron belly'. This 'blind No-God', which Carlyle saw as the appropriate deity of Utilitarianism and materialism, was certainly a poor alternative to the deposed Christian God. But the central fear here, such as that which weighed upon the young Mill, was that man had diminished to a mere puppet of the deterministic forces detected by modern science; that, as Dr Fitzpiers is reported to hold in *The Woodlanders*, 'no man's hands could help what they did, any more than the hands of a clock'. It was against such 'scientific' fatalism, so bound up with agnosticism, that Carlyle and other moralists reacted.

Indeed, the antimony of 'free-will' and 'philosophical necessity' was another aspect of the epochal self-division; and popular doctrines of moral freedom and 'self-help' were matched by popular conceptions of human automatism. Yet, although 'scientific', the ideology of determinism was often expressed mystically or phantasmagorically: one example is the threatening 'figure' which Hardy imagined as looming over and thwarting his life. An example in popular fiction is the dream which foretells the re-enactment of a murder by the murderer's son in Wilkie Collins's *Armadale* (1865). Certainly, the terrible fatality of heredity, which also figures in *Tess of the d'Urbervilles* and the works of George Eliot, for example, was a recurrent theme in Victorian fiction. Even more directly, however, the zombie image of human nature was reflected in the phenomena of mesmerism and somnambulism; thus we have the 'physiological experiment' with which Collins's best-known novel, *The Moonstone* (1868), climaxes, Franklin Blake being impelled by opium and hypnotic suggestion to re-enact his supposed theft of the diamond. Hardy, who used the sleepwalking motif in *Tess*, considered writing, in 1882, 'a history of human automatism, or impulsion'.

And thus it is not incidentally but as an expression of an epochal theme that the automaton image recurs in *The Return*. In the first bonfire scene at Mistover, Johnny Nunsuch 'seemed a mere automaton, galvanized into moving and speaking by the wayward Eustacia's will. He might have been the brass statue which Albertus Magnus is said to have animated just so far as to make it chatter, and move, and be his servant' (I:vi). The image is also applied to Venn in the gambling scene, in which he seems to resemble 'an automaton . . . a red-sandstone statue' (III:viii), and to function as an unconscious instrument of Wildeve's nemesis. Again, Mrs Yeobright's final, trance-like behaviour is like that of 'one in a mesmeric sleep' (IV:vi). However, subsuming all these symbolic details of determinism or abdication of free will is an implicit figure of Fate, most strikingly imagined by Eustacia as that 'Prince of the World, who had framed her situation and ruled her lot' (IV:viii).

The Disappearance of God

Yet, though his agnosticism often seems, like George Eliot's, to be bound up with the recognition of a determinism that deprives man of dignity and freedom, Hardy also sometimes seems to conceive of man as a victim of cosmic malevolence or even as a defiant Prometheus. This implication of a cosmic tyrant inconsistent with agnosticism or atheism was well expressed in Edmund Gosse's review of *Jude*: 'What has Providence done to Mr Hardy that he should rise up in the arable land of Wessex and shake his fist at his Creator?' Apparently Hardy, despite his agnosticism, still identified emotionally with the Romantic revolt against the Old Testament God of Vengeance – Blake's Nobodaddy. From his early years in London, Hardy also admired Swinburne, who continued to practise Romantic anti-Christianity and who managed to publish in *Atalanta in Calydon* (1865) the most notorious line in Victorian poetry:

> *The supreme evil, God.*

Both Shelley's *Prometheus Unbound* (1820), with its thesis of the moral inferiority of Omnipotence, and Swinburne's *Atalanta* are recalled in 'the President of the Immortals, in Æschylean phrase', who torments the heroine for 'his sport' in *Tess*. However, Hardy was also attracted by the more subtle anti-Christianity of Fitzgerald's *The Rubáiyát of Omar Khayyám* (1859), which, in the camouflage of a translation from medieval Persian, rejects Christianity as well as Victorian piety. In 1928, a few hours before his death, Hardy made his last gesture of defiance by having his wife read out this quatrain from *The Rubáiyát*:

> *Oh, Thou, who Man of baser Earth didst make,*
> *And ev'n with Paradise devise the Snake:*
> *For all the Sin wherewith the Face of Man*
> *Is blacken'd – Man's forgiveness give – and take!*

But as Hardy himself was well aware, there was a paradox or dilemma in this stance: how does one defy God after having ceased to believe in Him? Hardy's central statement of this dilemma is his poem 'Hap' (originally 'Chance'), which, though dated 1866, was first published in *Wessex Poems* (1898):

> *If but some vengeful god would call to me*
> *From up the sky, and laugh: 'Thou suffering thing,*
> *Know that thy sorrow is my ecstacy,*
> *That thy love's loss is my hate's profiting!'*

55

> *Then would I bear it, clench myself, and die,*
> *Steeled by the sense of ire unmerited;*
> *Half-eased in that a Powerfuller than I*
> *Had willed and meted me the tears I shed.*
>
> *But not so. How arrives it joy lies slain,*
> *And why unblooms the best hope ever sown?*
> *– Crass Casualty obstructs the sun and rain,*
> *And dicing Time for gladness casts a moan. . . . [original ellipsis]*
> *These purblind Doomsters had as readily strown*
> *Blisses about my pilgrimage as pain.*

Thus 'Hap', which Hardy seems to have preserved as a philosophical statement, testifies explicitly to the supersession of an anthropomorphic deity by a blind, cosmic 'Doomster'. In figures like the 'President of the Immortals' in *Tess* or the 'Prince of the World' in *The Return*, therefore, we are evidently meant to see ironic personifications of all the impersonal forces dooming human happiness. The irony is directed not, of course, at a literal, white-bearded God, as Gosse appeared to think, but rather at the pious illusion of Providence behind which 'crass Casualty' – or perhaps Carlyle's 'blind No-God, of Necessity and Mechanism' – lurks; that is, at the idea that a beneficent Creator could be compatible with the universe as modern man has learned to perceive it. Moreover, like Voltaire, Hardy is disallowing not only Christianity, but also the position of philosophical optimism that this is the best of all possible worlds and that particular evil and universal good are reconcilable.

In *The Return* the ultimate irony evoked by the apotheosis of destiny is dramatic; it reflects on the apostrophizer, Eustacia, herself. It is clear from the beginning that her Promethean defiance, her bitter awareness of 'the cruel satires that Fate [originally 'God'] loves to indulge in' (III:v), is a kind of self-delusion. In introducing Eustacia, the narrator tells us that her 'ever-growing consciousness of cruelty' and reproaches were 'directed less against human beings than against certain creatures of her mind, the chief of these being Destiny' (I:vii). Later, 'instead of blaming herself for the issue [of keeping out Clym's mother] she laid the fault upon the shoulders of some indistinct, colossal Prince of the World' (V:viii). Take finally her despairing soliloquy on Rainbarrow, spoken in the pouring rain just before she plunges into the weir:

'How I have tried and tried to be a splendid woman, and how destiny has been against me! . . . I do not deserve my lot!' she cried in a frenzy of bitter revolt. 'O, the cruelty of putting me into this ill-conceived world! I was capable of much; but I have been injured and blighted and crushed by things beyond my control! O, how hard it is of Heaven to devise such tortures for me, who have done no harm to Heaven at all.'

(V:vii)

Here the irony is dramatic inasmuch as there is no 'Heaven' either to pity Eustacia or to be affronted by her reproaches; as we know, there is only the unfeeling eternity typified by Egdon Heath. Yet this irony, as appropriate in a tragic medium, does not lessen our sympathy for Eustacia as a representative of aspiring humanity in an inhuman cosmos. But, to return to our main point, by putting together the implications of the poem 'Hap' and the dramatic irony that permeates *The Return*, we may conclude that Eustacia's persecutor, 'Fate', otherwise the 'Prince of the World', is to be taken as suffering mankind's subjective perception of an amoral, purposeless universe.

The Rejection of Meliorism

The Return, in particular the ironic portrayal of Clym, may also be taken to show that Hardy denied himself one of the principal consolations of agnosticism; unlike men like Spencer and Mill, he had little faith in the evolutionary meliorism, scientific programmes of moral and social progress, or secular religions with which it was hoped Christianity could be replaced. Anticipating Comte there had been Saint-Simon, the founder of French socialism, who had hoped to combine the brotherhood of Primitive Christianity with industrial and scientific progress. Influenced by Saint-Simon, Comte finally designed Positivism to be a 'Religion of Humanity' which would perfect human nature and society. Apparently, the 'ethical systems popular at the time' (III:ii) with which Clym became acquainted in Paris were those of Saint-Simon (who is invoked by name in *Far from the Madding Crowd*), other Utopian reformers such as Fourier and, of course, Comte. Clym's practice, in turning heath schoolmaster and later furze-cutter, reflects contemporary theories about the return to the simple life and the dignity of labour which, through thinkers like Carlyle and Ruskin, lead back ultimately to Saint-Simon; Clym's self-righteous adoption of the furze-cutter's garb recalls the Saint-Simonians' adoption of a worker's uniform. Clym's ideas are both altruistic and vaguely socialistic:

Clym Yeobright loved his kind. He had a conviction that the want of most men was knowledge of a sort which brings wisdom rather than affluence. He wished to raise the class at the expense of individuals rather than individuals at the expense of the class. What was more, he was ready at once to be the first unit sacrificed.

(III:ii)

Ironically, however, Clym's pretensions to secular sainthood are undercut by his own self-delusions and self-division. It is only by an almost wilful blindness that Clym could believe that Eustacia would serve as a teacher in a charity school, or that Egdon would welcome his reforms. The heath-folk's verdict on Clym's project is telling: ''Tis good-hearted of the young man ... But, for my part, I think he had better mind his business' (III:i). Nor does Clym's instinctive sympathy with the wildness of the heath or the inclemency of his passions square with the role of moral and social reformer in which he has cast himself. His opposition to Venn as being 'not quite ... gentleman enough' (VI:iii) to marry Thomasin is a particularly blatant contradiction of his ideals. All in all, Clym's practical failure as a reformer seems to represent the inevitable defeat of meliorism by 'the coil of things' (II:vi), the irreducibly unfavourable conditions of existence, which may even be fundamental in man's own nature. As various critics have suggested, Clym's story reflects Hardy's persistent scepticism regarding the inevitable progress taught by Positivism.

The Implications of Darwinism

Nor did Hardy find a basis for optimism in Darwinism, that other surrogate faith of his time. Darwin's conception of an inevitable evolution of life leading to ever higher forms but presumably culminating in man – or, more precisely, in the Victorian gentleman – offered a new reconciliation of natural law and progress, a kind of natural meliorism, that restored teleological purpose to a universe vacated by Christian Providence. Darwin found intimations of a biological providence even in the starvation, disease and predation that eliminate the unfit. Here, for example, is the vision of nature with which *On the Origin of Species* eloquently concludes:

It is interesting to contemplate an entangled bank, clothed with many plants of many kinds, with birds singing on the bushes, with various insects flitting about, and with worms crawling through the damp earth, and to reflect that these elaborately constructed forms, so different from each other, and dependent on each other in so complex a manner, have all been produced by laws acting around us ... Thus, from the war of nature, from famine and death, the most exalted objects which we are capable of conceiving, namely the production of the higher animals, directly follows. There is grandeur in this view of life, with its several powers, having been originally breathed into a few forms or into one; and that, whilst this planet has gone cycling on according to the fixed law of gravity, from so simple a beginning endless forms most beautiful and most wonderful have been, and are being, evolved.

Hardy later recalled that he had been 'among the earliest acclaimers of *On the Origin of Species*'; and given his obsessive concern with genealogy and heredity his interest in evolution is not surprising. A rather sinister reflection of evolution appears in *A Pair of Blue Eyes*, in the cliff-hanging scene already mentioned, in which Knight is rescued by Elfride just as he is slipping over the edge. As he clings to the cliff, Knight suddenly finds himself 'regarded' by 'the eyes, dead and turned to stone', of a fossil 'Trilobite' – 'a low type of animal existence' – embedded in the rock. Instantaneously, 'Time closed up like a fan before him', as he simultaneously sees cave men, mastodons, dinosaurs, 'fishy beings of lower development; and so on, till the lifetime scenes of the fossil confronting him were a present and modern condition of things'. As suggested by Knight's phylogenetic vision, Hardy's inferences from the phenomena of evolution and natural selection were less reassuring than Darwin's. In *The Woodlanders*, for example, there is a picture of nature in the depths of a wood which reads like a deliberate contrast to the exalted closing passage of *On the Origin of Species*:

On older trees . . . huge lobes of fungi grew like lungs. Here, as everywhere, the Unfulfilled Intention, which makes life what it is, was as obvious as it could be among the depraved crowds of a city slum. The leaf was deformed, the curve was crippled, the taper was interrupted; the lichen ate the vigour of the stalk, and the ivy slowly strangled to death the promising sapling.

Thus the 'Unfulfilled Intention' of Hardy's natural world contrasts starkly with Darwinian optimism about the direction of evolution; with Darwin's conviction that 'all corporeal and mental endowments will tend to progress towards perfection'. As shown by various notebook entries from the 1880s preserved in his autobiography, Hardy concluded that the evolution of human sensibilities and aspirations had been a cruel mistake of nature, 'that the human race is too extremely developed for its corporeal conditions, the nerves being evolved to an activity abnormal in such an environment . . . This planet does not supply the materials for happiness to higher existences'. In another notebook entry, Hardy seems to recall both Clym's contorting grief and Eustacia's final agony of despair: 'The emotions have no place in a world of defect, and it is a cruel injustice that they should have developed in it.' Darwin and Spencer had evidently failed to grasp – or refused to admit – that the evolution of consciousness in the 'higher existences', without a corresponding development of anaesthesia to the pains of existence, was a terrible defect in nature.

The Return must also be read in this context of defective evolution. Certainly, the associations and ecology of the heath, with its rare forms of life and vestiges of extinct races, are often recognizably Darwinian. For example, the conception of the struggle for existence and the inevitable extinction of less competitive forms, whether biological, social or economic, appears in the reddleman's introduction:

He was one of a class rapidly becoming extinct in Wessex, filling at present in the rural world the place which, during the last century, the dodo occupied in the world of animals. He is a curious, interesting, and nearly perished link between obsolete forms of life and those which generally prevail.

(I:ii)

On the heath, as on one of those genetically isolated islands explored by Darwin during his voyage on the *Beagle*, the evolutionary past projects preternaturally into the present; there is an uncanny telescoping of aeons, the same effect which had been strained in Knight's cliff-hanging vision. Thus the secluded hollow amidst the bracken, where Clym and Eustacia meet on a 'vaporously' warm and still day in early summer, 'seemed to belong to the ancient world of the carboniferous period, when the forms of plants were few, and of the fern kind; when there was neither bud nor blossom, nothing but a monotonous extent of leafage, amid which no bird sang' (III:v).

However, atavism on the heath is also cultural and psychic. The customs and superstitions of the heath-folk are vestiges of the primitive modes of thought and practices of their pagan ancestors. 'Indeed,' the narrator remarks, in reference to the 'May-revel',

the impulses of all such outlandish hamlets are pagan still: in these spots homage to nature, self-adoration, frantic gaieties, fragments of Teutonic rites to divinities whose names are forgotten, seem in some way or other to have survived mediaeval [originally 'Christian'] doctrine.

(VI:i)

Hardy may well have taken this theory of archaic cultural survival directly from its chief proponent, E. B. Tylor, the pioneer anthropologist. Clym's ironic question to his mother when they hear of the vicious witch-pricking inflicted upon Eustacia, 'Do you think I have turned teacher too soon?' (III:ii), may even have been suggested by the remark in Tylor's *Primitive Culture* (1871) that we 'cry out for more schoolmasters' when we hear of women still being persecuted as witches in English villages. In practices such as Susan's image-magic, the heath-folk exhibit vestiges of animistic beliefs; and here again Hardy seems to have been influenced by Tylor, who elaborates the theory – which he, in turn, had borrowed in part from Comte – that primitive man's world-view, like that of modern savages, was one of 'pure fetishism'. Here, by either 'animism' or 'fetishism', we mean the belief that man and all other creatures, natural phenomena or even artificial objects are alike in possessing souls as well as some degree of sentience. Such animism, which both Comte and Tylor held to be the earliest stage of religious development, may be detected, for example, in Christian's awe of the dice – 'That these little things should carry such luck, and such charm, and such a spell, and such power in 'em' (II:vii) – as well as in his fear of the adder: ' 'Tis to be hoped he can't ill-wish us!' (IV:vii).

But, on another level, the narrator's perception of the heath is itself animistic, inasmuch as it often deliberately goes beyond conventional poetic personification or what Ruskin called the 'pathetic fallacy' of ascribing emotions to nature. As has often been noted, the heath frequently appears as a living organism that impinges upon the lives of the characters. The scene of Eustacia's first vigil on Rainbarrow seems to intimate pantheism as she involuntarily merges her sighs with the whispery lament of 'the mummied heath-bells of the past summer':

'The spirit moved them.' A meaning of the phrase forced itself upon the attention; and an emotional listener's *fetishistic* [italics added] mood might have ended in one of more advanced quality. It was not, after all, that the left-hand expanse of old blooms spoke, or the right-hand, or those of the slope in front; but it was the single person of something else speaking through each at once.

Suddenly, on the barrow, there mingled with all this wild rhetoric of night a sound which modulated so naturally into the rest that its beginning and ending were hardly to be distinguished. The bluffs, and the bushes, and the heather-bells had broken silence; at last, so did the woman; and her articulation was but as another phrase of the same discourse as theirs. Thrown out on the winds it became twined in with them, and with them it flew away.

What she uttered was a lengthened sighing, apparently at something in her mind which had led to her presence here. There was a spasmodic abandonment about it as if, in allowing herself to utter the sound, the woman's brain had authorized what it could not regulate.

(I:vi)

Here we might speak, not only of another image of human automatism, but of Eustacia's mystical mergence with the heath; but at the same time it is clear that Hardy's transcendentalism is of a far darker variety than that of Wordsworth or Emerson. Moreover, Hardy's application of the anthropological term *fetishistic* to the scene reminds us that we are still in a Darwinian universe, that we have come full circle from primitive animism to the recognition of the evolutionary union of man and all organic nature. This is the uncanny recognition that grips Knight when, as he is slowly sliding to his own personal extinction, he comes face to face with a fossil ancestor.

However, as intimated by Knight's sinister recognition, in this 'world of defect' and evolutionary excess in sensitivity, man's fundamental unity with nature is one of suffering. In *The Return*, the voice speaking or wailing through all nature and reverberating in man's heart, as the echo of his own condition, is that of a universe of pain. We hear that figuratively animistic voice again, in another scene on Rainbarrow, as the wind in a mutilated thorn tree moans in harmony with the mutual despair of Eustacia and Wildeve: 'It was as if the night sang dirges with clenched teeth' (I:ix). Perhaps the most brutal image of natural torment appears in Clym's observation of the ravages of a storm in a plantation of young trees symbolically associated with Clym himself by their having 'been enclosed from heath lands in the year of his birth':

The wet young beeches were undergoing amputations, bruises, cripplings, and harsh lacerations, from which the wasting sap would bleed for many a day to come, and which would leave scars visible till the day of their burning. Each stem was wrenched at the root, where it moved like a bone in its socket, and at every onset of the gale convulsive sounds came from the branches, as if pain were felt.

(III:vi)

As one final illustration of this fatal identification of man and nature, we have Eustacia's last journey over Rainbarrow. Here the heath seems not only to participate in her disaster, stretching out tentacles to clutch at her ankles, but also to exhibit the debris of a Darwinian 'world of defect':

Skirting the pool [at Mistover] she followed the path towards Rainbarrow, occasionally stumbling over twisted furze-roots, tufts of rushes, or oozing lumps of fleshy fungi, which at this season lay scattered about the heath like the rotten liver and lungs of some colossal animal.

(V:vii)

One final point on the evolutionary context of *The Return* remains to be made, namely that Clym's disproportioned mind and tendency to melancholia reflect not only Hardy's own idiosyncratic views on mental overdevelopment and racial exhaustion, but also the paradoxical fear among Darwinians themselves that advanced civilization breeds morbid refinement, hyperaesthesia and sterility. In this sense, Clym's characterization anticipates the so-called 'Decadence', the literary movement which was influenced by biological theories of 'higher' degeneracy; and we shall return to Hardy's connection with the Decadence. But Clym 'already showed that thought is a disease of flesh' (II:vi); he prefigures the spiritual weariness that 'must ultimately enter so thoroughly into the constitution of the advanced races' (III:i). At the same time, as his mother confirms in warning Eustacia to beware of his temper, Clym is ever liable to revert to the native type – his father, the Egdon farmer, had been 'rough as a hedge' (II:iii) – but this is part of Clym's characteristic self-division. In the Darwinian context, we seem finally to see Clym, in his introspective pain, as personifying evolution morbidly conscious of itself.

The Conflict of 'Hellenism' and 'Hebraism'

We leave Darwinism now in order to look at other ideas in ethics and aesthetics which influenced *The Return* though we shall find Darwinian implications in other ideological systems, so central was the evolutionary thesis to the age. One of these other influences is Matthew Arnold's antithesis of Hellenism and Hebraism, which various critics have detected in *The Return*, where it seems to be associated with an implicit conflict between paganism and Christianity. In *Culture and Anarchy* (1869), Arnold defined the intellectual principle, which he called 'Hellenism', and the moral principle, which he called 'Hebraism', as the two fundamental and often opposing forces in British culture and society. In his own words, 'The uppermost idea with Hellenism is to see things as they really are; the uppermost idea with Hebraism is conduct and obedience ... The governing idea of Hellenism is *spontaneity of consciousness*; that of Hebraism, *strictness of conscience* [his italics].'

Arnold made three additional points of relevance here. First, he noted that Hebraism, in the form of Christianity, had superseded Hellenism in the ancient world because the Hellenic conception of human nature as semi-divine had proved to be premature and untenable. Second, Arnold observed that the revival of Hellenism in the Renaissance, though glorious, 'had, like the anterior Hellenism of the Pagan world, a side of moral weakness and of relaxation or insensibility of the moral fibre'. Lastly, he pointed out that Hebraism, in the form of Puritanism, had been 'the reaction in the seventeenth century of the conscience and moral sense of our race, against the moral indifference and lax rule of conduct which in the sixteenth century came in with the Renascence'. Although Arnold believed Hellenism to be inherent in the Indo-European race and Hebraism in the Semitic, he found the Anglo-Saxons, by some special dispensation of the law of heredity, especially endowed with this Semitic principle.

When we look at *The Return* in the light of Arnold's antithesis of Hebraism and Hellenism, we may immediately recognize Clym as predominately a 'Hebraic' type. He is certainly, in the terms of Arnold's description of Hebraism, 'severely preoccupied with an awful sense of the impossibility of being at ease in Zion'; moreover, Hardy identifies him with Arnold's patron saint of Hebraism, St Paul. Hardy also contrasts Clym's attributes with 'the Hellenic idea of life' (III:i). Still, it is possible to see in Clym 'spontaneity of consciousness' as well as 'strictness of conscience'. In taking 'ennoblement' for his 'text' and arguing for 'the possibility of culture before luxury' (III:ii), Clym sometimes seems not to be St Paul at all but rather an Arnoldian advocate of 'sweetness and light', as culture is defined in *Culture and Anarchy*. Moreover, like Angel Clare, Clym seems to be intellectually a free-thinker and morally a Puritan – not an uncommon double identity at the time – and he seems to be attracted as much by Eustacia's defiance and nihilism as by the dark splendour of her hair and eyes. Clym's passion for her shows that he does not achieve, until too late, that self-conquest which Arnold saw as central to Hebraism. In short, we may see the influence of Arnold's antithesis in Clym's self-division and in his unreconciled moral, intellectual and aesthetic urgings.

On the other hand, Eustacia, who prefers Saul to Paul, seems to be the very antitype of Hebraism. Eustacia and, to a lesser extent, Wildeve, though not apparently representative of intellectual Hellenism, do represent a spirit of presumption, self-indulgence, and even amorality associated by Arnold with Hellenism. Eustacia is obviously linked, as in the 'Queen of Night' chapter in Book I, with the overweening grandeur of Hellenic antiquity; indeed, this chapter seems to be deliberately antithetical to the introductory description of Clym. Of course, through her Greek father Eustacia literally descends from the prototypal Hellenes, in keeping with Arnold's emphasis on the moral characteristics of race. Moreover, Eustacia is also associated with the pre-Christian spirit of the heath. Thus she and Wildeve surrender themselves to Dionysian exhilaration in the 'gipsying' when 'Paganism was revived in [the dancers'] hearts, the pride of life was all in all, and they adored none other than themselves' (IV:iii). Eustacia's symbolic conflict with Christianity is dramatized in the mummer's play on Christmas Day, in which, in the role of the Turkish Knight, the infidel champion, she is ritually slain by St George. Hence, in the view of some readers, we have in *The Return* an allegory of the defeat and destruction of pagan heroism by modern Hebraism.

Such allegorical conflict may seem far removed from the original thesis of Arnold, who was, in fact, cautiously arguing for less Hebraism and more Hellenism. Still, Clym's disastrous championing of Hebraism and the destruction of Eustacia and Wildeve could be taken as illustrations of Arnold's argument. At the same time, Clym's hopeless division between moral and intellectual or aesthetic principles might be seen as Hardy's ironic view of that synthesis of Hebraism and Hellenism which Arnold prescribed for national improvement. For Hardy, Arnoldian liberalism could only be another foredoomed form of meliorism.

Ethical and Aesthetic Views of Life

However, in this ideological context, we must finally see the main thematic antithesis in *The Return* not only as a conflict between 'Hebraic' Christianity and 'Hellenic' paganism, but also as an opposition between an ethical view of life, as represented – however imperfectly – by Clym, and an aesthetic view, as represented by Eustacia. In fact, the latter opposition was central to the age; and it may be seen as subsuming Arnold's antithesis of Hebraism and Hellenism. A dissociation of the ethical and the aesthetic was already apparent in Byronism, and we may note that this dissociation becomes explicit in Eustacia: 'As far as social ethics were concerned Eustacia approached the savage state, though in emotion she was all the while an epicure' (I:x). But such a dissociation was, of course, by no means an exclusively 'Anglo-Saxon' phenomenon. Indeed its classic, if at the time untranslated, analysis appears in Kierkegaard's *Either/Or* (1843), in which the aesthetic alternative is manifest not only in the artistic monstrosity of a Nero – who would have a child killed before its mother's face in the hope that her despair might express a new model of tragic passion – but also in any Byronic demand for self-realization. Thus, in the aesthetic view, a person with an inclination to be, say, a Don Juan or a Faust or a corsair must cultivate that inclination in order to become something striking and thereby escape the ennui of ordinary existence. However, the ethical development of the self, according to one of the personae in *Either/Or*, requires the suppression of Promethean aspiration and the acceptance of ennui. Kierkegaard's formulations, though they are a parallel not a source in relation to Victorian literature, help us to place Eustacia's yearning to be a Helen or a Cleopatra in this context of existential aestheticism. In concluding that the end of the aesthetic view of life must necessarily be nullity and despair, *Either/Or* also anticipates Eustacia's suicide when she realizes that she cannot become 'a splendid woman' (V:vii).

Of course, as a thematic antithesis to Eustacia's hunger for splendour, her 'aesthetic' selfishness, we have Clym's altruistic asceticism. Although the narrator tells us that Clym 'advocates aesthetic effort and deprecates social effort', this statement occurs in the context of Clym's preaching of 'the possibility of culture before luxury' (III:ii); the word *aesthetic* here, therefore, denotes 'uplifting'. In the same chapter the narrator explains that Clym's 'local peculiarity was that in striving at *high thinking* he still cleaved to *plain living* [italics added]', the italicized phrases coming from Wordsworth's sonnet 'In London, September, 1802', which is an attack on luxury and ostentation:

> *We must run glittering like a brook*
> *In the open sunshine, or we are unblest:*
> *The wealthiest man among us is the best:*
> *No grandeur now in nature or in book*
> *Delights us. Rapine, avarice, expense,*
> *This is idolatry; and these we adore:*
> *Plain living and high thinking are no more.*

Thus Wordsworth's abhorrence of jewellery as a symbol of false values seems to have influenced Hardy's conception of Clym, in particular Clym's revulsion from 'the flashy business' of 'trafficking in glittering splendours with wealthy women and titled libertines, and pandering to the meanest vanities' (III:ii). Hence he 'stigmatized' Eustacia's tastes 'as vain and luxurious' (IV:viii). But Clym's renunciation of splendour also includes what Kierkegaard would have called the aesthetic view of life and of the self. As Clym tells Eustacia when she chides his resignation:

Now, don't you suppose, my inexperienced girl, that I cannot rebel, in high Promethean fashion, against the gods and fate as well as you. I have felt more steam and smoke of that sort than you have ever heard of. But the more I see of life the more do I perceive that there is nothing particularly great in its greatest walks, and therefore nothing particularly small in mine of furze-cutting.

(IV:ii)

In this fundamental antithesis of the ethical and the aesthetic, a representative Victorian ideologue is Ruskin. In *The Two Paths* (1857), Ruskin, unconsciously recalling Kierkegaard's Nero, associated aestheticism with barbarism; the practice of art for its own sake he found '*destructive both of intellectual power and moral principle* [his italics]'. Here Ruskin's main example was the ornate, arabesque architecture of India, which he contrasted with Wordsworthian simplicity and correlated with the fiendish treatment of British women during the Indian Mutiny. However, this observation of 'the apparent connection of great success in art with subsequent national degradation' also applied to the Renaissance: 'The paintings of Raphael and [Michelangelo] gave force to the falsehoods of superstition, and majesty to the imaginations of sin'. Hence Ruskin championed the Pre-Raphaelite school of English painters, who proposed to return to the austerity and morality of artistic representation that had supposedly prevailed before the decadence of the High Renaissance.

The Influence of Walter Pater's Aestheticism

On the other hand, the aesthetic view found an eloquent champion in Pater, whose *Studies in the Renaissance* (1873) had a greater influence on *The Return* than anything by either Arnold or Ruskin. Pater gracefully ignored their strictures on the Renaissance; moreover, in his Conclusion he enunciated an Epicurean and evidently non-Christian ethos, in which the highest good is refinement and intensity of experience, whether emotional, intellectual or aesthetic. We have only a limited interval of consciousness between birth and the grave, Pater observes; 'our one chance lies in expanding that interval, in getting as many pulsations as possible into the given time'. The passions, the 'ecstasy and sorrow of love', may provide this 'quickened, multiplied consciousness'; but 'the poetic passion, the desire of beauty, the love of art for art's sake, has most; for art comes to you professing frankly to give nothing but the highest quality to your moments as they pass, and simply for those moments' sake'. 'To burn always with this hard, gemlike flame, to maintain this ecstasy, is success in life.'

Pater contrasted the serenity of classical art to the exquisite subtlety, tortured introspection and mysticism of High Renaissance art. But he found it inevitable that the 'Hellenic ideal, in which man is at unity with himself' (Pater uses the word *Hellenic* in its original meaning of 'classical Greek'), should give place to the self-division and inner conflict of advanced sensibility; otherwise, man would have been in danger of an ennui of perfection. For Pater, Renaissance art was not so much a rebirth of Hellenism as a marvellous post-Hellenic distillation – the culmination of a millennium of moral and aesthetic experience. Here, for example, is the most celebrated interpretation in Pater's book (the passage which Hardy seems to be recalling in the 'Queen of Night' chapter in *The Return*), the description of da Vinci's portrait of an enigmatically smiling lady, *La Gioconda* (also known as *Mona Lisa*):

The presence that thus rose so strangely beside the waters, is expressive of what in the ways of a thousand years man had come to desire. Hers is the head upon which all 'the ends of the world are come', and the eyelids are a little weary. It is a beauty wrought out from within upon the flesh, the deposit, little cell by cell, of strange thoughts and fantastic reveries and exquisite passions. Set it for a moment beside one of those white Greek goddesses or beautiful women of antiquity, and how would they be troubled by this beauty, into which the soul with all its maladies has passed? All the thoughts and experience of the world have etched and moulded there, in that which they have of power to refine and make expressive the outward form, the animalism of Greece, the lust of Rome, the reverie of the middle age with its spiritual ambition and imaginative loves, the return of the Pagan world, the sins of the Borgias. She is older than the rocks among which she sits; like the vampire, she has been dead many times, and learned the secrets of the grave; and has been a diver in deep seas, and keeps their fallen day about her; and trafficked for strange webs with Eastern merchants; and, as Leda, was the mother of Helen of Troy, and, as Saint Anne, the mother of Mary; and all this has been to her but as the sound of lyres and flutes, and lives only in the delicacy with which it has moulded the changing lineaments, and tinged the eyelids and the hands.

Thus Pater's portrait of a portrait becomes the epitome of his whole conception of the Renaissance, while his prose style recreates in itself the supposed High Renaissance sensibility so abominated by Ruskin and the Pre-Raphaelites. The Decadents seized on Pater's apparent attribution of moral ambiguity and hyperaesthesia to advanced culture; and Pater's 'La Gioconda', like his Conclusion, became a vital document of English Aestheticism.

Pater's stylistic influence in *The Return* has often been noted; the influence of his ideas less so. We might note, first of all, that Hardy's allusions to Renaissance painters in *The Return* seem to echo the aesthetic sympathies of Pater. Eustacia is associated with Raphael in one of the mumming scenes; and, at the same time, Raphael's superiority to his predecessor Perugino is affirmed (II:v). More significantly, we can probably take Pater's *Renaissance* as the most immediate source of Eustacia's embodiment both of an aesthetic view of life and of the sensuous beauty associated with Hellenism on many Renaissance canvases. Eustacia 'was in person full-limbed and somewhat heavy; without ruddiness, as without pallor; and soft to the touch as a cloud' (I:vii). Her dread of ennui and hatred of her provincial imprisonment perhaps owe something directly to Emma Bovary; but her 'super-subtle epicurean heart' (I:xi), her attraction to 'the wisdom of Carpe diem' (III:v), her longing for 'music, poetry, passion, war, and all the beating and pulsing that is going on in the great arteries of the world' (IV:vi) and her preference for 'a blaze of love, and extinction' to 'a lantern glimmer of the same which should last long years' (I:vii) all follow from Pater's hedonistic Conclusion. At the same time, Eustacia's incarnation of the instinctive paganism of the heath, where she figures, for the heath-folk, almost as a local Hecate, may also owe something to Pater's conception of a universal pagan survival. In this context we have already mentioned the influence of Comte and Tylor; but Hardy is also likely to have had in mind Pater's reflections on 'a universal pagan sentiment, a paganism which existed before the Greek religion, and has lingered far onward into the Christian world, ineradicable, like some persistent vegetable growth, because its seed is an element of the very soil out of which it springs'. Still, the most recognizably Paterian influence in *The Return* remains the opulence of imagery and conceit, the 'Asiatic prose' – to borrow Oscar Wilde's phrase – of the 'Queen of Night' chapter. Take, for example, the following passages from that chapter:

[Eustacia] had Pagan eyes, full of nocturnal mysteries, and their light, as it came and went, and came again, was partially hampered by their oppressive lids and lashes; and of these the under lid was much fuller than it usually is with English women. This enabled her to indulge in reverie without seeming to do so: she might have been believed capable of sleeping without closing them up. Assuming that the souls of men and women were visible essences, you could fancy the colour of Eustacia's soul to be flame-like. The sparks from it that rose into her dark pupils gave the same impression.

Her presence brought memories of such things as Bourbon roses, rubies, and tropical midnights; her moods recalled lotus-eaters and the march in 'Athalie'; her motions, the ebb and flow of the sea; her voice, the viola. In a dim light, and with a slight rearrangement of her hair, her general figure might have stood for that of either of the higher female deities. The new moon behind her head, an old helmet upon it, a diadem of accidental dewdrops round her brow, would have been adjuncts sufficient to strike the note of Artemis, Athena, or Hera respectively, with as close an approximation to the antique as that which passes muster on many respected canvases.

(I:vii)

This portrait, which has often been taken as one of the most absurd of Hardy's purple passages, seems to have been meant as a deliberate merging of style and content, in the manner of Pater. Here the immediate effect is an impression of dark exoticism which is to be Eustacia's leitmotiv. However, when we compare Hardy's 'Queen of Night' closely with Pater's 'La Gioconda', we find a disparity both of image and idea. Pater's portrait is that of a jaded aesthete and mystic, whose 'eyelids are a little weary', whose sophistication has passed far beyond either indignation, rapture or despair. But Eustacia, though 'her moods recalled lotus-eaters', is neither a Decadent *femme fatale* nor a vampire. Her essential attributes are those of Hellenic paganism, and her beauty recalls 'one of those white Greek goddesses or beautiful women of antiquity' with whom Pater contrasts his symbolic figure. Unlike his post-Hellenic 'Lady Lisa', Eustacia is still capable of tragic feeling, as if she were a queen in captivity; 'the shady splendour of her beauty was the real surface of the sad and stifled warmth within her' (I:vii). We may conclude that Eustacia represents a Hellenism at once anachronistic and stifled;

that she is modelled as if in deliberate contrast to the 'modern' dispassion and resignation of Pater's 'La Gioconda'.

We can also see the general influence of Pater's impressionistic prose-portraiture in the delineation of two other symbolic faces in *The Return*; namely, the opening description of Egdon Heath, 'A Face on Which Time Makes But Little Impression', and in the later set-piece description of Clym's 'modern', prematurely worn countenance. But though this adoption of Paterian style and impressionistic technique, like Hardy's apparent admiration for High Renaissance painters, suggests a tendency to aestheticism, we must hasten to add that such a tendency is usually undercut by irony. Even in the 'Queen of Night' chapter there is a deflation of rhetoric alien to Pater: 'Eustacia Vye was the raw material of a divinity . . . She had the passions and instincts which make a model goddess, that is, those which make not quite a model woman' (I:vii).

However, let us now look at the specific influence of Pater in the set-piece description of Clym. Clym's portrait, which constitutes a thematic contrast to Eustacia's, is rendered in two instalments. Our first look at his face is through the anxious eyes of the disguised Eustacia, who has just enacted the death of the Turkish Knight at the hands of St George. In the firelight the returned native's appearance is a 'spectacle . . . in Rembrandt's intensest manner. A strange power in [Clym's] appearance lay in the fact that, though his whole figure was visible, the observer's eye was only aware of his face':

The face was well shaped, even excellently. But the mind within was beginning to use it as a mere waste tablet whereon to trace its idiosyncrasies as they developed themselves. The beauty here visible would in no long time be ruthlessly overrun by its parasite, thought, which might just as well have fed upon a plainer exterior where there was nothing it could harm. Had Heaven preserved Yeobright from a wearing habit of meditation, people would have said, 'A handsome man.' Had his brain unfolded under sharper contours they would have said, 'A thoughtful man.' But an inner strenuousness was preying upon an outer symmetry, and they rated his look as singular . . . He already showed that thought is a disease of flesh, and indirectly bore evidence that ideal physical beauty is incompatible with emotional development and full recognition of the coil of things. Mental luminousness must be fed with the oil of life, even though there is already a physical need for it; and the pitiful sight of two demands on one supply was just showing itself here.

As for his look, it was a natural cheerfulness striving against depression from without, and not quite succeeding. The look suggested isolation, but it revealed something more. As is usual with bright natures, the deity that lies ignominiously chained within an ephemeral human carcase shone out of him like a ray.

(II:vi)

The portrait, or rather impressionistic reflection, is completed in the opening of Book III:

In Clym Yeobright's face could be dimly seen the typical countenance of the future. Should there be a classic period to art hereafter, its Pheidias may produce such faces. The view of life as a thing to be put up with, replacing that zest for existence which was so intense in early civilizations, must ultimately enter so thoroughly into the constitution of the advanced races that its facial expression will become accepted as a new artistic departure. People already feel that a man who lives without disturbing a curve of feature, or setting a mark of mental concern anywhere upon himself, is too far removed from modern perceptiveness to be a modern type. Physically beautiful men – the glory of the race when it was young – are almost an anachronism now; and we may wonder whether, at some time or other, physically beautiful women may not be an anachronism likewise.

The truth seems to be that a long line of disillusive centuries has permanently displaced the Hellenic idea of life, or whatever it may be called. What the Greeks only suspected we know well; what their Aeschylus imagined our nursery children feel. That old-fashioned revelling in the general situation grows less and less possible as we uncover the defects of natural laws, and see the quandary that man is in by their operation.

(III:i)

In this composite picture of Clym as 'a modern type', a post-Hellenic thinker, we can again perceive the general influence of Pater's method of symbolic portraiture, his merging of style and idea in order to create an epitome of a particular sensibility or philosophy. Moreover, when we place Clym's portrait beside Pater's 'La Gioconda', we may immediately notice various correspondences in detail. The central metaphor in Clym's delineation – that of an inner spirit working outward, wasting the beauty of his countenance and rendering his look 'singular' – seems to derive, *mutatis mutandis*, from the disturbing beauty of Lady Lisa, which 'is a beauty wrought out from within upon the flesh'. 'Etched and moulded' by 'strange thoughts and fantastic reveries and exquisite passions', her plastic face seems to have suggested Clym's hieroglyphic face, which 'the mind within was beginning to use . . . as a mere waste tablet whereon to trace its idiosyncrasies as they developed'.

Clym's involuntary demonstration 'that ideal physical beauty is incompatible with emotional development' is also anticipated by Lady Lisa's morbid beauty, 'into which the soul with all its maladies has passed'. Pater adds that the 'beautiful women of antiquity' would be 'troubled' by Lady Lisa's presence; and, indeed, in the mumming scene, Eustacia 'was troubled at Yeobright's presence' (II:vi). Hardy apparently derived from Pater the idea that Hellenic art portrays an ideal physical beauty

71

untroubled by introspection or by that 'mutually destructive interdependence of spirit and flesh' (III:i) evident in Clym. According to Pater, 'The Greek mind had advanced to a particular stage of self-reflexion, but was careful not to pass beyond it.' Greek art, consequently, 'has not yet become too inward; the mind has not yet begun to boast of its independence of the flesh; the spirit has not yet absorbed everything with its emotions, nor reflected its own colour everywhere'. It was Christianity, with its asceticism and mysticism, Pater continues, that discredited the physical body and the joy of life, introduced the conflict of soul and body, and thus prepared the ground for the strange flowering of Renaissance art. The pathology of self-division had only just begun to appear in Greek tragedy. 'Greek sensuousness, therefore, does not fever the blood; it is shameless and childlike.' How anachronistic, Pater concludes, is the Hellenic spirit in 'our alien, modern atmosphere'. In short, the themes expressed in Clym's portrait, of the regrettable triumph of spirit over body and of the anachronism of physical beauty, seem to be directly derived from Pater. Likewise Paterian in source is Hardy's conception of the permanent 'displacement' of 'the Hellenic idea of life' as well as his conception of the relative innocence and underdeveloped sensibility of the Greeks. In Hardy's words again, 'What the Greeks only suspected we know well; what their Aeschylus imagined our nursery children feel.'

However, it is also clear, even in the portrait of Clym, that Hardy has transformed Pater's two central antitheses in this context, that of Hellenism and modernism and that of the soul and the body, and adapted them to his own purposes. In the first place, Hardy, far more than Pater, seems to have seen the opposition between Hellenism and modernism as an evolutionary differentiation between 'younger races' and 'advanced races'. As we may infer from our previous discussion of Darwinism and racial degeneracy, Hardy's differentiation here would be twofold. First, from the standpoint of mere racial longevity, 'that zest for existence which was so intense in early civilizations' must naturally contrast with the attenuation of aged cultures. Secondly, as an inescapable consequence of the misguided direction of evolution towards ever more refined nerves and acute brains, advanced races must be infinitely more cognizant than early races of 'the defects of natural laws' as well as more sensitive to the pains of existence. Hence, what 'Aeschylus imagined our nursery children feel'.

This pathology of advanced sensibility is not inconsistent with the philosophy of the Decadence; Hardy later came near to writing a Decadent fantasy himself in his penultimate novel, *The Well-Beloved* (1892), the only one of his novels to feature an artist as protagonist. Moreover, the Aeschylean child spoken of in general terms in the portrait of Clym – and adumbrated in that 'sad,' 'old-fashioned child', Johnny Nunsuch –

becomes in *Jude the Obscure* the terrible Father Time, who converts his parents' closet into a lethal chamber, in order to put himself and his siblings out of their misery. In his diagnosis of Father Time's case,

The doctor says there are such boys springing up amongst us – boys of a sort unknown in the past generation – the outcome of new views of life. They seem to see all its terrors before they are old enough to have staying power to resist them. He says it is the beginning of the common universal wish not to live.

However, while Pater attributed the passing of the spirit of Hellenism, with its revelling in the joy of life, to the Christian transcendence of the body, Hardy attributed 'the beginning of the common universal wish not to live' to the evolutionary advance of perception and the 'full recognition of the coil of things'.

And thus, as must necessarily follow from his theory of the hypertrophy of modern man's sensibilities, Hardy's sense of the interrelationship of spirit and body was much darker than Pater's. Whereas Pater saw beauty and the triumph of aestheticism in the working of spirit upon the body, Hardy saw affliction and doom: 'Mental luminousness must be fed with the oil of life.' In Clym, 'thought' is a 'parasite', 'a disease of flesh', 'preying upon an outer symmetry'; and the imagery of biological pathology here reflects again the evolutionary bias of Hardy's thinking. Given that Darwinian universe of pain composing his world-view, Hardy was bound to reverse Pater's assumptions regarding the nature of happiness in the modern world; to deplore that cultivation of sensation and heightening of feeling, that Epicurean philosophy of 'getting as many pulsations as possible into [our] given time'. As the portraits of the doomed Eustacia and the hyperaesthetic Clym clearly indicate, Hardy, despite his indebtedness to Pater, could no more have entertained hedonism or aestheticism than he could have accommodated meliorism in his world-view.

'The Ache of Modernism'

Clym's representation of the ethical view of life is closely bound up with that 'strange power' of reflection which illuminates his face and which may be taken both as evolution morbidly conscious of itself and as 'modern' man's consciousness of the hopeless unfitness of things. 'I got up every morning and see the whole creation groaning and travailing in pain', Clym tells his mother. Necessarily, then, his primary ethical aspiration is 'to buckle to and teach [men] how to breast the misery they are born to' (III:ii). But even the Epicureanism of Eustacia, whom we have spoken of as representing an 'aesthetic' view of life, is infected by the 'universal wish not to live' or by what is called 'the ache of modernism' in *Tess of the d'Urbervilles*. Even Pater had detected an essential sadness in paganism; and Clym finds that his beloved's 'eyes seem heavy' at the very moment of exaltation, Eustacia explaining that this heaviness 'arises from my feeling sometimes an agonizing pity for myself that I ever was born' (III:iv). Indeed, the mumming scene in which Clym's fascination begins foreshadows the scene in which Angel is moved to discover that the apparently innocent Tess, too, feels 'this hobble of being alive'. In the earlier scene, Clym, having divined that the Turkish Knight is a woman incognito, is drawn to question her:

His eyes lingered on her with great interest. 'Do girls often play as mummers now? They never used to.'
 'They don't now.'
 'Why did you?'
 'To get excitement and shake off depression,' she said in low tones.
 'What depressed you?'
 'Life.'
 'That's a cause of depression a good many have to put up with.'
 'Yes.'

(II:v)

Of course, Eustacia's response to this existential depression is ultimately suicide; Clym's response is his fruitless ethical aspiration, which culminates in catastrophe and a too late resignation. In view of this 'ache of modernism' or recognition of life's fundamental hopelessness, which paralyzes both protagonists, both the ethical and the aesthetic views of life must be presented ironically. Thus the pessimistic vision of life usually associated with the fatalistic workings of plot in Hardy's tragic fiction is first fully articulated in *The Return*.

In conclusion, we may emphasize that Hardy's sense of existential alienation, the sense of a character, alone, in stark opposition to a hostile or uncaring universe – as portrayed in Eustacia's final soliloquy – makes *The Return* a very atypical Victorian novel and gives it a distinctly modern tone. Quite overshadowing Clym's sense of social ethics, this conception of character ultimately disjointed from social relationships contrasts sharply with the social realism, the teeming, interrelated world of a novel by Thackeray or Trollope. At the same time, however, we must note that the 'ache of modernism' attributed to Angel and Tess but already apparent in *The Return*, though certainly a theme idiosyncratic in Hardy, was an explicit expression of an existential unease and doubt widely implicit or suppressed in Victorian thought. The Decadence was another expression of the spiritual malaise that seemed to afflict Victorian culture at its apogee.

3. Plot, Structure and Form in *The Return of the Native*

In this section we examine structure and organization in *The Return*, considering such elements as plot, character, setting and point of view. Of course, these structural elements are dynamically interrelated; consideration of one of them inevitably involves the others. It should also be noted at the outset that structural devices may be either formal and explicit or informal and implicit. An example of highly formal structures in *The Return* is the organization of the narrative into books and chapters; an example of highly informal structure, the implicit observance of the 'Aristotelian' unities of place and time proper to tragic drama. Our eventual concern is the extent to which novel form is superseded by tragic form in *The Return*.

Background to Hardy's Conception of Plot

Let us review the understanding of plot current in the nineteenth century, an understanding – still dominant today – that was Aristotelian in basis. In his *Poetics* Aristotle, who was referring primarily to tragedy, tersely defined plot as the ordering of events. However, the *Poetics* implies that plot, which Aristotle declared to be the most essential element or 'soul' of composition, is the structuring of events or action into a cause-and-effect sequence. Hence, true plot is to be distinguished from mere story or episodic plot, in which there is no logic of development in the sequence of events. Aristotle said that true plot has unity of action; i.e. there is no irrelevant incident in the sequence, and it is impossible to displace any single event without upsetting the whole plot. Furthermore, according to Aristotle, plot is essentially mimesis, i.e. imitation of human action; and this mimesis should be consistently plausible in terms of the logic of causation as well as in moral terms. Therefore, there should be neither an unprepared catastrophe, nor a *deus ex machina* ending, nor a good man punished. Coincidence, however, is admissible if it has the appearance of purpose; Aristotle instanced a murderer killed by a statue of his victim which fell on him. Finally, the so-called Aristotelian unities, as reformulated in the seventeenth century, include, in addition to unity of action, unity of time, which restricts the duration of the action of a tragedy to one day, and unity of place, which restricts the action of a tragedy to one physical setting.

The Aristotelian emphasis on plot as the main structuring element in literary form had been crucial in the development of the novel from the episodic prose romance. Apparently the pioneer English novelists found the principle of structural integrity offered by plot congenial to their mechanistic world-view. While the 'novels' of Defoe were still markedly episodic and relatively formless, lacking even chapters, his immediate successors, Richardson and Fielding, were masters of plot development. Thus Coleridge found Fielding's *Tom Jones* (1749) to rank with Sophocles' *Oedipus Rex* in perfection of plot. The Victorian novelists, then, had before them a neoclassical model of plot in the eighteenth-century novel. Even the rather portentous organization into 'books', in the manner of Fielding's imitation of epic form, may be found not only in *The Return*, but also in novels by Dickens and Eliot. However, in the Victorian novel, unity of action was often compromised by the voluminosity encouraged by both the three-volume format and serial publication. A commercially successful serial might be extended despite the limitations of the original plot, while organization into monthly numbers often introduced an episodic tendency in the narrative. The concomitant proliferation of characters, ramification of sub-plots, uneven development of main plot, and editorial interference combined to produce the 'loose, baggy monster' deplored by Henry James.

Among Victorian novelists, Hardy is distinguished by his concern with unity of plot. Despite Hardy's concessions to his editors, *The Return* is unusual, for the time, in its austerity of form and plot, its compelling unity of action. Hardy's consciousness of the aesthetic implications of plot was already evident in *The Poor Man and the Lady*, even though it was defiantly subtitled *A Story with No Plot*. For what Hardy seems to have been defying in *The Poor Man* was not so much the necessity of plot as the conventions of the portrayal of society, conventions which had become the touchstone of verisimilitude. In striking down the heroine just after her marriage to the protagonist, Hardy had also defied the principle of moral probability. In other words, he had rebelled against the role of Providence, a role which the novelist, ever since Fielding, had been expected to assume towards his characters.

However, in his other apprentice novel, *Desperate Remedies*, Hardy deliberately imitated the plot conventions of the 'sensation-novel'. In *Desperate Remedies* these conventions, which are merely exaggerations of those of Victorian fiction in general, include the 'long and intricately inwrought chain of circumstances'; the reliance on coincidence, mystery, surprise and machination; and the ultimate vindication of innocence and punishment of guilt. In Collins's *The Woman in White*, Hardy's particular model, the plot centres upon the conspiracy to confine Laura for life in a madhouse, in substitution for an escaped inmate – actually her illegitimate half-sister, Anne – who has conveniently died while a fugitive and whose resemblance to Laura permits the substitution. Here Collins's Providence is doubling as Nemesis, for it is the original sin of Laura's father in begetting Anne that 'unerringly' leads, 'in the long chain of circumstances', to the plot against Laura, in keeping with the moral that 'The sins of the fathers shall be visited on the children.' Nevertheless, Laura is providentially rescued, while her persecutors are destroyed by no official justice but, again by the workings of an apparent Nemesis. Moreover, in both *The Woman in White* and *The Moonstone*, Collins employs a 'documentary' method of narration, including letters, journal extracts and depositions as well as assiduous attention to setting, dates and times; in short, he manipulates the conventions of realism in order to give the appearance of probability to an inherently improbable plot. We may recognize the influence of this documentary verisimilitude also in *Desperate Remedies*.

However, with regard to his evolving conception of plot, perhaps Hardy's most significant borrowing from Collins was what we may call the manipulation theme, in which one character, whether a villain or a benefactor, mysteriously controls or distorts the life of another. In *The Woman in White*, Count Fosco marries Laura to a scoundrel, and he finally strips her of both identity and freedom. But the manipulation theme was common beyond the bounds of the sensation-novel; we may also find it, for example, in Emily Brontë's *Wuthering Heights* (1847), Meredith's *Richard Feverel* (1859), and Dickens's *Great Expectations* (1861). At times, the conspiracy to control a life becomes virtually synonymous with the plot of the novel. By the same token, the manipulator himself may usurp the role of destiny or God, as if, in the words of *Richard Feverel*, 'one human being might almost impersonate Providence to another'. In *Desperate Remedies*, it will be recalled, Cytherea is the victim of a plot hatched by Miss Aldclyffe, who is spoken of as 'a Lachesis or Fate'. Indeed, in manipulating Cytherea's life, Miss Aldclyffe and Manston sometimes seem to be playing the role assigned to malign Fate in Hardy's tragic novels; even coincidence and the elements seem to favour their schemes, as when a thunderstorm traps Cytherea in Manston's house.

Hardy's adoption of the manipulation theme in *Desperate Remedies* is another indication of his developing subversion of Providence as an element in plot. Of course, like Laura, Cytherea is, after all, rescued from the villain and reunited with the hero. But behind Hardy's simulation of Providence and Nemesis – Manston hangs himself in prison – we catch glimpses of inscrutable forces at work. One such glimpse comes midway through the novel when Cytherea misinterprets the series of sinister coincidences linking herself and Miss Aldclyffe:

> But when three such events coincide without any apparent reason for the coincidence it seems as if there must be invisible means at work ... From these premises, [Cytherea] proceeded to argue like an elderly divine on the designs of Providence which were apparent in such conjunctions.

Thus in *Desperate Remedies* the convention of coincidence is already becoming self-consciously ironic and suggestive not of God but of Hap.

In *A Pair of Blue Eyes* Hardy takes his irony at the expense of Providence even further. In retrospect from the ending, we can appreciate the tacit sarcasm of the narrator's earlier observation when Elfride nearly falls from a church tower: 'By what seemed the special interposition of a considerate Providence she tottered to the inner edge of the parapet instead of to the outer.' In fact, the ill-starred girl is pursued by ominous 'conjunctures' which parody Collins's providential coincidences. For example, when the grief-stricken Hartright visits Laura's grave whom should he meet there but Laura herself, who has just escaped from her keepers. On the other hand, in *A Pair of Blue Eyes* the surprise is that Elfride is dead; and her two lovers, arriving to propose to her, instead attend her entombment. Unlike *The Woman in White* and *Desperate Remedies*, there is no conspirator in *A Pair of Blue Eyes*; but at times it seems as if that role has been taken by Fate itself.

Certainly, Elfride's destruction is exceedingly arbitrary and hardly related to any conceivable chain of causation or retribution other than cosmic malevolence. Nevertheless, we have in *A Pair of Blue Eyes* something approaching the basic plot pattern of Hardy's mature novels beginning with *The Return*. That basic pattern includes features such as the 'long and intricately inwrought chain of circumstances', the series of ironic or mysterious coincidences, the interlocking fates of characters, and the permeating theme of fatality, all of which were apparently inherited directly from the sensation-novel. However, Hardy's typical plot is tragic in the sense that the protagonist is destroyed or defeated as the inevitable consequence of a chain of events originally set in motion by his own actions or aspiration. And yet Hardy is not a fatalist in any ordinary sense. Unlike Collins's puppets, Hardy's characters are free; but their freedom is impotent. At the same time, this fatality, unlike that inherent in the plots of Collins, Dickens or Eliot, derives neither from Providence, nor from moral purpose, nor yet from a pattern of retribution such as the visiting of the sins of the fathers upon the children (though the last named principle frequently figures as a rationalization or red herring in Hardy's fiction). On the other hand, an Anti-Providence also proves to be an illusion of subjectivity in Hardy's mature novels.

We are left with the sense that Hardy's plot, in the final analysis, reflects the same purposeless, alien universe predicated by his 'post-Hellenic' thought. Critics such as Ian Gregor and J. Hillis Miller have drawn attention to the analogical or metaphysical function of Hardy's plot. According to Gregor, in a novel by Hardy the plot is 'mimetic of the plot of the universe', coincidence being the deliberate and ironic intersection of these two different plots. We must conclude that the fatality inseparable from Hardy's fictional plot is by design mysterious and perhaps ultimately unsusceptible to rational analysis, in analogy with a universe inscrutably hostile to man, 'that universe', in the words of Hardy's General Preface to the Wessex Edition, 'concerning which Spencer owns to the "paralysing thought" that possibly there exists no comprehension of it anywhere'.

Levels of Plot in *The Return of the Native*

Hardy's novels were originally criticized for their supposed improbability of plot, character and setting, i.e. their lapses in conventional verisimilitude. On the other hand, critics now commonly observe that Hardy's fiction is not realistic in intention; that Hardy was writing tragedies, ironic romances or allegories rather than novels; and that he deliberately neglected rationality in plot as well as the psychological or social analysis cultivated in their several ways by contemporaries like Trollope, Eliot and James. At the same time, Hardy is still frequently accused of confusing the realistic and the nonrealistic modes.

In our analysis of plot and structure, we shall assume first of all that *The Return* cannot be isolated from that context of realism which frames all nineteenth-century literature. Certainly, Hardy later wrote that '"realism" is not Art'; 'Art is a disproportioning – (i.e. distorting, throwing out of proportion) – of realities, to show more clearly the features that matter in those realities.' Yet he was well aware that in order to be published at all he had at least to simulate the realistic conventions that obtained in all sub-genres of the Victorian novel. In various respects, especially in his re-creation of the details of rural life, Hardy seems even to have considered himself a realist. In his General Preface, Hardy

79

classified his novels, according to their degree of verisimilitude, into three groups. The first category he called 'Novels of Character and Environment', including *The Return, The Mayor of Casterbridge* and the other obviously great novels. He placed *A Pair of Blue Eyes* in the second group, 'Romances and Fantasies'; and he consigned *Desperate Remedies* and *Ethelberta* to a third group, 'Novels of Ingenuity', which 'show a not infrequent disregard of the probable in the chain of events'. This classification indicates that Hardy was conscious of the tension between realistic and nonrealistic tendencies in his work, and his giving pride of place to 'Novels of Character and Environment' is an acknowledgement of the quasi-scientific claims of contemporary realism. At any rate, we shall deal with the problem of realism in *The Return* by assuming that its plot functions on more than one level; that in plot and structure we have again the principle of simultaneity.

In effect, the plot of *The Return* is at once realistic, tragic and mythic. At the surface or literal level, the plot functions realistically, at least in the sense conventionally understood by Hardy's editors, reviewers and readers. This is the level of interpretation represented, for example, by the magazine illustrations of the novel, by chapter titles, and by the reviewers' strictures. Underlying this realistic level is Hardy's tragic plot with its implicitly dramatic organization and its figurative observance of the Aristotelian unities. To borrow the term of the 'myth critic', Northrop Frye, we might say that tragic form has been 'displaced' at the explicit level by the conventions of realism. However, at an even deeper and more fundamental level we have the mythic or archetypal plot, upon which Hardy's modern interpreters increasingly focus. At this mythic level, the plot of *The Return* is supposed to merge with the archetypes – such as the renewal of communal life through sacrificial death – underlying all literature, drama and mythology. Here conscious structure is replaced by symbolic action, as in the mummers' play or in Eustacia's 'labyrinthine' dream of dancing with a masked partner, in both of which ritualistic episodes she unconsciously acts out her own destruction. Let us, for now, give one brief example of the simultaneity of the three levels. In the realistic plot, Eustacia is a gifted but selfish young woman stifled and driven to her death by an adverse environment. At the tragic level, she is a Promethean protagonist who chooses death over captivity. As a mythic figure, she is a sacrificial victim associated with such other scapegoats as Guy Fawkes, Mary Stuart, the Wandering Jew, the Renaissance witches and the mummers' Turkish Knight.

Unity of Action in the Realistic Plot

Book I

We begin our analysis with the explicit or realistic level of plot. On this level the immediately apparent organizing theme is the very conventional one of troubled courtship and rivalry in love. In Book I the rising action and complication centre on the entangled love affairs of Thomasin, Venn, Eustacia and Wildeve. The narrative begins *in medias res* as the faithful Venn carries Thomasin in his van to Blooms-End, following her humiliation by Wildeve's invalid licence. From the heath-folk's gossip we learn more about the troubled relations of Thomasin and Wildeve, whose banns had been dramatically forbidden by Mrs Yeobright. Presently we learn of the liaison that had existed between Wildeve and Eustacia – before he jilted her for Thomasin – by overhearing their rendezvous at Mistover Knap. Through yet another flashback, i.e. Thomasin's old letter which we read over Venn's shoulder, we are informed that Venn is Thomasin's rejected suitor. Thus Hardy relies on the convention of the triangle to structure relationships. In fact, in Book I we have two triangles, one centring on Thomasin, and the other on Wildeve, who is torn between Eustacia and Thomasin. Of course, in Venn's selfless love for Thomasin we have Hardy's favourite theme of a man aspiring to the hand of a woman of higher status.

Conflict and intrigue arise directly from these ill-starred love affairs. Mrs Yeobright, who had vehemently opposed Wildeve's courtship of Thomasin, is now as determined, for the same reasons of family pride, to see that he honours his engagement to her niece. Venn disinterestedly comes to Mrs Yeobright's assistance, attempting to induce Eustacia to relinquish her hold over Thomasin's 'chameleon' fiancé, in a scene which anticipates Melbury's unsuccessful intercession with Felice in *The Woodlanders*. (Hardy's characters are evidently ignorant of breach-of-promise suits and horsewhipping, two accepted methods of dealing with unfaithful fiancés in Victorian fiction.) In Venn's detective-like operations we can detect the vestiges of the manipulation theme, a theme which loomed larger in the Ur-version of *The Return*. Originally, it will be recalled, Eustacia had been conceived of as Thomasin's diabolical persecutor; and a trace of this malignity appears in the satisfaction she evidently takes in Thomasin's suffering. Venn certainly thinks of Eustacia 'as a conspirator against . . . Thomasin's happiness' (I:ix). For his own part, Venn assumes the role of a local providence for his beloved;

81

'to be in Thomasin's heath, and near her, yet unseen' (I:ix) is his remaining pleasure.

In relation to these lines of conflict and intrigue, we may note the emergent pattern of ironic accident, coincidence, and foreshadowing. Indeed, the story effectively begins with Thomasin's happening to meet Venn, whom she has not seen since his proposal to her two years before, on the very morning of her cancelled wedding. Thus it is by extraordinary coincidence that Venn becomes reinvolved in Thomasin's life; and it is a second accidental meeting that day involving Venn and Thomasin – their overtaking by the inquisitive Captain Vye on the road home – which informs Eustacia of the cancellation and leads, in turn, to her bonfire summons to Wildeve. For, by another coincidence, the day of the intended wedding is also Guy Fawkes Day, the traditional bonfire of which has previously served as a lovers' signal for Eustacia and Wildeve. Ironically, it is when Wildeve happens to go on the heath in order to deliver a charitable bottle of wine to an ailing cottager that he is decisively attracted by Eustacia's fire. By yet a fifth interlocking coincidence that day, the substance of what Eustacia and Wildeve say to each other beside the bonfire is reported to Venn by its stoker, little Johnny Nunsuch, who happens to tumble into Venn's camp. Of course, the initiation of this particular train of events is Wildeve's error with the licence, the kind of apparently casual slip with grave consequences which may also be seen in Fanny's fatal mistake of the church appointed for her wedding to Troy in *Far from the Madding Crowd.*

This shaping of events into a pattern of apparent purpose or fatality occurs without great strain on credulity or on the presentational conventions of realism, because Hardy's grasp of character and event, of locale and setting, is so sure. At least temporarily, we accept the narrative on a realistic level as the chapter titles invite us to do. Foreshadowing reinforces a sense of inevitability, as in Eustacia's remark about the hateful heath: '''Tis my cross, my shame, and will be my death!' (I:ix). A passage in Thomasin's letter to Venn, 'I always put you next to my cousin Clym in my mind' (I:ix), foreshadows the later, implicitly triangular relations of the three. Book I closes with the news of Clym's impending return, Captain Vye remarking, significantly for Eustacia's 'Parisian desires', that the promising Clym has been living all these years 'in that rookery of pomp and vanity, Paris' (I:xi).

However, in reviewing Book I we can perceive a more fundamental organizing theme than that of unhappiness in love. This more basic pattern, in which the theme of sexual love is subsumed, is that of life frustrated and oppressed by adverse circumstance and environment.

Indeed, such a pattern is typical of the realism and naturalism – the theme of 'Character and Environment' – that dominated late-nineteenth-century British fiction. In Book I it is oppressive social convention – personified, to some extent, by Mrs Yeobright – which promotes disastrous mismatches; which separates Thomasin and Venn, who are natural mates, and insists on Thomasin's being made an honest woman of by the philandering Wildeve. It is clear also that Eustacia's neurotic indulgence in passion springs from her frustration at the circumstances which ironically confine her, a native of that gay coastal resort Budmouth and a natural Parisienne, among 'a parcel of cottagers' on 'netherward Egdon'. Wildeve, too, 'was brought up to better things' (I:iii); he has sunk from engineer to innkeeper. But the most vivid emblem of life distorted by misfortune is Venn's reddle-stained clothing and skin, a degradation which he embraced after his rejection by Thomasin.

In keeping with this dominant theme of life immured by circumstance – the heath is repeatedly referred to as Eustacia's 'gaol' – we have the 'architectural' structure of Hardy's plot, that construction of interlocking events and consequences which has been both criticized as mechanical and praised as well-built. Moreover, a block-like design is apparent in Hardy's organization of the narrative into books, though book divisions and titles are conventional in the Victorian novel. The title of Book I, 'The Three Women', focuses our attention on the vital female characters who will inspire the action; but, by emphasizing the static element of character, this title also makes us think of Book I as the foundation of the narrative structure. In contrast, the title of Book II, 'The Arrival', focuses attention on the forward movement of plot; in particular, it realizes the 'return' of the title of the novel.

We should also note here that in introducing the complication of Clym's return Hardy was drawing on literary convention. A character's return to the scenes of his childhood is a stock situation in Victorian fiction. A suggestive example here is another of Ainsworth's Gothic romances, *Rookwood* (1834). In fact, Chapter 7 of Book I of *Rookwood* is entitled 'The Return'; and it depicts the return to his ancestral mansion, following his father's death, of the idealistic Rookwood heir, who is not only in love with his first cousin but is also to quarrel violently on a matter of principle with his haughty and worldly mother. Another example of a strong-willed mother bitterly disappointed by her son's return from abroad appears in George Eliot's *Felix Holt* (1866). Moreover, like Clym, Harold Transome in *Felix Holt* pursues Oedipal probings into a secret better left undiscovered.

Book II

Book II, then, introduces the primary complication of Clym's return. Eustacia has heard Clym tantalizingly associated with Paris, and by typical coincidence she overhears the heath-folk say that she and he 'would make a very pretty pigeon-pair' (II:i). She is 'led on' to her adventure at Blooms-End as the Turkish Knight by the coincidence that her admirer Charley is one of the mummers. Here again we have the strong impression of fatality, of character being determined by event. In fact, the narrator compares Eustacia's 'predetermination' to fall in love with Clym to pathological cases of suggestibility. Book II reaches its carefully prepared climax in the mumming scene in Chapter 6, in which Clym finally appears in full view, 'palpably' affecting the overwrought Eustacia. As the other mummers have already guessed her true sex, Clym also divines it, leading to the dialogue in which Clym seems to be affected in his turn by the strange depression of the masked girl. Their interview in the moonlight has a trance-like, revelatory quality, recalling the other allusions to mesmeric compulsion.

Eustacia's encounter with Clym leads directly to a restructuring of triangles. Ironically, Eustacia, who has, like the dog in the manger, been grudging Wildeve to Thomasin, must now fear Thomasin as a potential rival for Clym. By a further irony, Thomasin is the more 'interesting' or attractive because of the very pallor and suffering attributable, in part, to Eustacia. Having formerly rejected his overtures, Eustacia now forms a 'coalition' with Venn in order to 'help on' Thomasin's marriage to Wildeve. Accordingly, she dispatches, via the insolent medium of Venn, her dismissal of Wildeve, piquing him, as she intends, into claiming Thomasin at last under the delusion that he is 'wringing' Eustacia's heart. 'Who was to know that [Eustacia] had grown generous in the greediness of a new passion, that in coveting one cousin she was dealing liberally with another, that in her eagerness to appropriate she gave way?' (II:vii). Book II closes with the wedding of Thomasin and the out-manoeuvred Wildeve, Eustacia unexpectedly appearing, to the bridegroom's discomposure, as witness, while Venn looks on from the gallery. From this strange scene, which assembles, for the first time, all of the members of the original two triangles, Clym is absent, having been ignorant of Thomasin's dilemma. However, Eustacia's presence is consistent with the shadow which she casts over the marriage.

Book III

In Book III, 'The Fascination', Clym at last takes centre stage, Venn having vanished from Egdon immediately after reporting Thomasin's wedding to Mrs Yeobright. We infer that Clym's curious inaction in his cousin's affairs – as her nearest male relative it was his place to bring Wildeve to book – has resulted, in part, from the preoccupation underlying his return. Clym too, in giving up his career in Paris and returning to the heath, is struggling against the doom of circumstances, against 'that waggery of fate which ... banished the wild and ascetic heath lad to a trade whose sole concern was with the especial symbols of self-indulgence and vainglory' (III:i). The initial conflict in Book III is that between Clym's aspiration and a restrictive conventionality represented by his mother, who has also taken this role in her niece's affairs.

However, coincidence and the concatenation of events soon lead to a renewal of the theme of sexual love. Even as Clym is arguing with his mother about his intention to challenge circumstance, news comes of Eustacia's pricking that morning in church, where Eustacia, not normally a churchgoer, had presumably gone in the hope of seeing Clym. This report of the 'cruelly treated girl' instantly arouses Clym's interest in her. Thus Eustacia's intention in entering Blooms-End in disguise – her only visit there – works on, as if independently. By a second coincidence that day, Clym is invited to help recover the well bucket at Mistover; he is now almost as eager to meet the 'witch-lady' as she had been to see him. The absence of Captain Vye, who has gone to prosecute Susan, facilitates the *tête-à-tête* between Clym and Eustacia, in whom Clym recognizes not only a 'romantic martyr to superstition', but also 'the melancholy mummer he had conversed with under the full moon' (III:ii). Eustacia's burning of her hand on the well rope leads to her showing Clym also the mark left by Susan's stocking-needle, a wound which seems to ornament 'her round white arm ... like a ruby on Parian marble' (III:iii). Clym looks 'at the scarlet little puncture as if he would like to kiss it and make it well', for his fascination by Eustacia clearly begins with her appeal as a victim. This aspect of sexuality in *The Return*, which may also be seen in Clym's supposed susceptibility to the distressed Thomasin, might now be called sadomasochistic; but it must be kept in mind that such a confusion of suffering and sexual attraction, like the motif of attraction between first cousins, is too common in Victorian fiction to be attributed to the personal obsession of any particular author. But the point to be emphasized here is that Clym's falling in love partakes of that fatality which is continually transcending consciousness and intention. We can trace even the pricking itself, which originally attracts Clym to Eustacia, back to Wildeve's invalid licence and the resulting bonfire signal, for it was Eustacia's forcing Johnny Nunsuch to stoke that fire that first led his mother to suspect her of witchcraft.

Clym's attraction to Eustacia provokes even bitterer conflict with his mother, who has feared this very fascination, and whose hostility to her son's beloved seems to combine family pride with an irrational jealousy. Clym himself, despite his growing passion for Eustacia, is torn between filial and sexual feeling. In the pattern of natural pairing among the characters, Thomasin, by temperament and nature, obviously pairs with Venn, and Eustacia with Wildeve, leaving Clym with his mother. Eustacia certainly regards Mrs Yeobright as her greatest rival, and in their later 'rencounter' demands to know whether her inimical mother-in-law will 'not come and drag [Clym] out of my hands?' (IV:i). Books III and IV are accordingly dominated by the incestuous triangle of Eustacia, Clym and his mother.

In Chapter 4 of Book III, at the exact midpoint of the novel, Clym and Eustacia, after less than three months' acquaintance, ominously plight their troths, under a lunar eclipse, on Rainbarrow. But this pledge brings no satisfaction, though both lovers delude themselves considerably – Eustacia in thinking that Clym will, after all, establish her in Paris, Clym in persistently regarding Eustacia as a suitable matron for his future boarding-school. Yet Eustacia is full of foreboding about their future; and Clym, in his heart, realizes that his struggle against circumstance is virtually doomed from the start:

Three antagonistic growths had to be kept alive: his mother's trust in him, his plan for becoming a teacher, and Eustacia's happiness. His fervid nature could not afford to relinquish one of these, though two of the three were as many as he could hope to preserve.

(III:iv)

In the event, Clym's engagement rapidly leads to a breach with his mother and his removal to the cottage at Alderworth, thus forging a major link in the chain of events resulting in Mrs Yeobright's death.

The wedding day of Clym and Eustacia does not pass without a sign of the imminent reinvolvement in the bride's life of Wildeve, to whom the news of her approaching marriage has brought 'a curious heartache': 'The old longing for Eustacia had reappeared in his soul: and it was mainly because he had discovered that it was another man's intention to possess her' (III:vi). As if to tease this longing, it is on the very evening of Eustacia's wedding that another series of coincidences – and gambler's luck – allows Wildeve temporarily to intercept the hundred antique guineas, Mrs Yeobright's 'family jewels', which she charges Christian to deliver in equal shares to Clym and Thomasin. Having won the coins from Christian, Wildeve apparently intends to frustrate Mrs Yeobright by presenting Clym's share to Eustacia as a token of his continuing feeling for her. No sooner does Wildeve have the guineas in his hands, however, than Venn, who has not been seen on the heath since Thomasin's wedding, startlingly appears; and of course he wins the guineas from Wildeve, in a continuation of the midnight gambling scene.

As much as any scene in *The Return*, this phantasmagoric duel with the dice-box between the phlegmatic reddleman and the choleric innkeeper strains the verisimilitude of realistic fiction – the scene seems to belong, in spirit, more to the folktale or the ballad – for in this scene Hardy's symbolism comes close to the surface. Lighted by thirteen glowworms, after a moth puts out Wildeve's candle, the dicing ritualizes the irony and caprice of fate. First Christian, then Wildeve, and finally Venn is favoured – 'Fortune had unmistakably fallen in love with the reddleman tonight' (III:viii). But we no more doubt the appropriateness of Venn's victory than we believe that his extraordinary run of luck will avert ultimate misfortune. In fact, Venn, though he has overheard Wildeve's conversation with Christian, has missed the point that half of the guineas are meant for Clym; he delivers them all to Thomasin that same night, with ultimately disastrous results.

In the incident of the guineas, with which Book III climaxes, we see again the fatal pattern of events apparently overwhelming human intention and intervention. Mrs Yeobright's intention in sending the guineas to Clym and Thomasin is conciliatory; the gift is a sign 'showing how far she was from bearing [Clym] ill-will' (III:vii). This benevolent aim is frustrated by accident, by Christian's weakness, and by Wildeve's spite. When Venn, resuming his role of providence, attempts to put things right, he only furthers the misdirection. Mrs Yeobright, understanding from Christian that Wildeve has won the guineas, and ignorant that Venn has delivered them all to Thomasin, comes to believe that Wildeve has mischievously given Clym's share to Eustacia. This series of misunderstandings leads directly to the bitter quarrel between Eustacia and her mother-in-law in Book IV.

Book IV

In Book IV, as suggested by its ominous title 'The Closed Door', the pattern of fatality closes in. In Chapter 1, 'The Rencounter by the Pool', the only meeting between Clym's mother and his wife quickly degenerates into unforgivable recriminations. Conscious that her mother-in-law may be aware of her past relations with Wildeve, Eustacia is quick to resent Mrs Yeobright's enquiry about a gift of money from him; Mrs Yeobright is equally quick to see hateful insolence in the younger woman. Thus Clym's hope of a reconciliation between them soon turns to despair; and this despair is compounded by Eustacia's demanding, as a direct consequence of the quarrel, to move to Paris. Two of Clym's aims, his mother's confidence and his wife's happiness, have now, like the guineas, gone awry; and his third aim, his plan to become a teacher, is presently blocked by the inflammation of his eyes brought on by the study necessary to carry out that plan. With additional irony, Clym has also become blind to the frustration which is increasingly wracking Eustacia. His resignation exasperates her, and he fails to appreciate what an effect his turning furze-cutter will have upon her. Eustacia is being pro- gressively reduced to the state in which she might defy her marriage vow. Link by link, the concatenation of circumstances and events leads to disaster.

Coincidence also persists in Book IV. Happening to hear Clym sing a French song while cutting furze, Eustacia is first moved to 'sick despair' and then stung into a mood of ironic merriment in which she sets out to attend a 'gipsying' on the heath. By chance Wildeve is also there. They dance, and the circumstances awaken the old attachment: 'The dance had come like an irresistible attack upon whatever sense of social order there was in their minds, to drive them back into old paths which were now doubly irregular' (IV:iii). A chance meeting, then, leads directly to the adulterous triangle of Books IV and V. The members of this triangle seem about to be assembled in one scene when Wildeve, walking Eus- tacia home after the 'gipsying', sees Clym and Venn approaching. But Wildeve slinks off across the heath before he can be seen by the half- blind Clym, thus initiating, by one guilty impulse, the pattern of evasion and deception in which Eustacia is soon to become trapped. Wildeve's action here foreshadows his back-door exit from the cottage at Alder- worth when Mrs Yeobright knocks unavailingly for admission.

But Venn has seen Wildeve slipping away from Eustacia's side on the path to Alderworth; and the reddleman is soon back 'into the old track of manoeuvring on Thomasin's account' (IV:iv), and devising 'coun- termoves' to her errant husband's moves towards Eustacia. We now realize even more clearly, however, that Venn is pitted not simply against Wildeve, but against fate. As in the affair of the guineas in Book III, Venn's 'providential' interventions in Book IV only hasten disaster. His 'rough coercion' causes Wildeve to abandon his nightly haunting of the cottage at Alderworth, with the result that Wildeve pays his daytime visit to Eustacia, resulting, in turn, in her fatal hesitation in opening the door to Clym's mother.

Thus, in Mrs Yeobright's unfortunate 'journey across the heath', we see benevolent intention thwarted by an extraordinary yet not unbelievable sequence of coincidence. Encouraged by Venn, from whom she now learns of Clym's eye disease and recourse to furze-cutting, Mrs Yeobright sets out determined to forgive all past offences and misunderstandings. Clym too is now eager to heal the breach with his mother. In the event, the 'conjuncture' of Wildeve's presence and Eustacia's embarrassment, which Mrs Yeobright's own suspicion has helped to create, lead to Eustacia's failure to open the door immediately to the unexpected knock of her mother-in-law. The crueller accident of Clym's calling out 'Mother' in his sleep, thereby convincing Eustacia that he is opening the door himself, ensures the mother's exclusion. Moreover, by ill chance Mrs Yeobright knows that Clym is at home, having happened to see him ahead of her on the path to the cottage, just as she sees Eustacia peering at her from the side window. Consequently, Mrs Yeobright retraces her steps across the heath, too aggrieved at what she takes to be Eustacia's cruelty and her son's rejection to realize the danger of continued exertion under the blazing August sun. The ubiquitous Venn is now nowhere to be seen; and Mrs Yeobright meets only that bird of ill omen, Johnny Nunsuch. To complete this worst possible combination of mishaps, an adder strikes the sufferer, apparently just as she is sinking from sunstroke. When Clym stumbles upon his mother after nightfall, having set out, too late, to seek reconciliation at Blooms-End, she is already incoherent and beyond hope.

Yet the workings of ill chance that day continue. After Clym, still ignorant of his mother's attempted visit, sets off for Blooms-End, Eustacia learns from her grandfather that Wildeve has inherited a fortune through the sudden deaths of all his relatives. 'What a fool you were, Eustacia! . . . in not sticking to him when you had him', Captain Vye chides, perhaps voicing her own thoughts. Going out upon the heath in order to ponder this irony, Eustacia happens to meet whom else but Wildeve, who adds to her sense of 'the satire of heaven' by explaining that he now intends to settle in Paris. The pair are about to part, not without a gallant kissing of Eustacia's hand by Wildeve, when they happen upon the turf-shed where Mrs Yeobright, attended by Clym, Thomasin and the heath-folk, lies dying. Remaining in the shadows outside the shed, Eustacia and Wildeve are just in time to witness Mrs

Yeobright's death as well as Clym's prostration as a result of Johnny Nunsuch's happening to repeat in his hearing the dead woman's last message: 'She said I was to say . . . she was a broken-hearted woman and cast off by her son' (IV:viii).

This ominous scene at the turf-shed, with which Book IV concludes, momentarily assembles all the main characters except Venn, though the shed wall and the shadows divide Eustacia and Wildeve from the others, while the door of death soon closes upon Mrs Yeobright. This scene, then, parallels the scene in the cottage at Alderworth, which had assembled the members of both the incestuous and the adulterous triangles, though Clym had been, characteristically, unconscious throughout and his mother had been divided from the others by the door. In emphasizing the secretive pairing of Eustacia and Wildeve as well as the unconsciousness or exclusion of the Yeobrights, both scenes illustrate Hardy's use of choreographic groupings to represent relationships among characters, just as the recurrent pattern of crossed paths graphically represents the characters' cross-purposes. We may also note in the earlier scene, in which Eustacia and Wildeve gaze upon the sleeping Clym, a foreshadowing of the mortuary scene, at the end of Book V, in which Clym displays the apparently slumbering lovers. In fact, Clym and Wildeve are to meet face to face, both being fully conscious, only once, in the scene of catastrophe at the weir. Indeed, members of a triangle seldom appear together. Clym, Wildeve and Eustacia are never knowingly together; nor Clym, Eustacia and Mrs Yeobright; nor Wildeve, Eustacia and Thomasin, except in the climactic wedding scene; nor Wildeve, Thomasin and Venn.

Book V

The title of Book V, 'The Discovery', might be called Aristotelian, since *discovery* is the word usually used to translate *anagnorisis*, Aristotle's term for the protagonist's recognition of some vital implication of the plot hitherto hidden from him. Clym's inevitable discovery of Eustacia's role in his mother's death comes in Chapter 2, suspense having been heightened by foreshadowing and a series of dramatic ironies. Here the bitterest irony is Clym's throes of self-reproach, 'which had become as dreadful to [Eustacia] as the trial scene was to Judas Iscariot' (V:i). Having failed to confess before, she is now committed to a deceptive silence, in which she is encouraged by Wildeve. Moreover, Clym's grief seems to replace affection for his wife; in the grave, Mrs Yeobright is an even more powerful rival. Obsessed by the mystery of his mother's death,

Clym begins his detective-like investigation. Venn intervenes, again with unintended consequences, for it is his assurance that Mrs Yeobright was coming, on the day of her death, to forgive her son and daughter-in-law that drives Clym to undergo the pain of questioning Johnny Nunsuch. From this strange child, who had earlier served as Venn's informant, Clym discovers that Eustacia had a gentleman caller within while keeping out his mother; but he too hastily infers her guilt of adultery.

The ensuing confrontation between Clym and his wife in Chapter 3, the turning point or crisis of the novel, has been foreshadowed in the quarrel in the opening chapter of Book IV, in which Mrs Yeobright warned her defiant daughter-in-law of Clym's harsher nature; and in calling Eustacia a whore, Clym seems to reincarnate and exaggerate his mother's instinctive hostility towards her 'supplanter'. The psychological realism of this scene can hardly be doubted, though the dialogue is stylized and is more in keeping with the tragic level of plot. At any rate, Clym's outburst is decisive in dooming Eustacia. Crushed, despite her pride, by Clym's relentlessness, she takes refuge at Mistover Knap, where the final scenes of her life are to be played out. Clym will not see her face again until after her death.

It is Eustacia's exile at Mistover that gives rise to the final train of events. The narrative has now covered nearly a year; and the 5th of November is approaching again, though Eustacia in her despair is scarcely aware of the date. In an attempt to divert her, Charley, the Captain's stable-lad, who has resumed his role as her worshipper, kindles a great bonfire by the pool, the trysting place, on the evening of the 5th. Here again events seem to have a momentum and purpose that has broken free from human intention. By lighting the Guy Fawkes bonfire, Charley inadvertently summons Wildeve, who arrives fired by his old ardour for Eustacia. His unexpected presence and tenderness move Eustacia to accept his offer of assistance should she resolve on flight.

Even while Eustacia and Wildeve are having what proves to be their last words together, Thomasin, who has become aware of her husband's renewed attraction to Eustacia, is urging Clym to forgive his wife. Clym, now living at Blooms-End where he makes a religion of his mother's memory, has in fact been hoping that Eustacia will return to him of her own accord. Persuaded by Thomasin, he writes a conciliatory letter to Eustacia; but, characteristically, he delays sending it until the following day. Thus the mutual failure of Clym and his mother to communicate when both were eager for reconciliation is recapitulated by Clym and his wife. But here Hap again takes a hand, for when Clym does finally dispatch his letter on the afternoon of the 6th, various accidents prevent

Eustacia from getting it. This miscarriage of the letter is particularly unfortunate, because Clym's violence on the day of his discovery has convinced Eustacia, in the absence of any subsequent sign from him, that she will never be forgiven and 'would have to live on as a painful object, isolated, and out of place' (V:vii).

Thus the stage is set for the catastrophe, to which the concluding three chapters of Book V are devoted. Still in despair but desperately clutching at the hope of escape offered by Wildeve, Eustacia, having signalled her intention to him with a flaming furze bough, slips away from Mistover late on the evening of the 6th, in order to meet Wildeve on the road below the Quiet Woman Inn. As if representing the doom of circumstances, a raging storm pelts the fugitive, who pauses on Rainbarrow as the full implications of her dilemma dawn upon her. Lacking money, she must either go abroad as Wildeve's dependent mistress or remain at home as Clym's disgraced wife – an unendurable humiliation in either case. It is through this eminently practical dilemma that the cosmic malignancy perceived by Eustacia is manifested. Again we have a simultaneity of realism and symbolism, the latter represented by the storm as well as by the voodoo effigy which Susan torments while Eustacia, exposed on Rainbarrow, sinks under the weight of adversity. Chapter 7 closes with Eustacia crouched upon the soaked heather, and she now disappears from our sight until her plunge into the weir in Chapter 9. There is an element of ambiguity in this fatal plunge since the narrator never says whether it is intentional or accidental. We shall return presently to this ambiguity in Eustacia's death, for it is part of the general problem of intention in *The Return*.

While Eustacia is pursuing her fatal course across the heath, the alarm has been raised for her as for an escaping prisoner. We then have the frantic crisscrossing of the heath by all the characters, suspense being sustained by Eustacia's disappearance from our view following her soliloquy on Rainbarrow. In Chapter 9 the characters' paths converge on the weir, near which Clym and Wildeve finally come face to face, in full realization of their relationship to each other – though even here Wildeve is obscured behind the gig lamp. At the moment of their instantaneous confrontation, Eustacia plunges into the 'boiling cauldron': and her lovers follow her in – Wildeve precipitantly and Clym cautiously. Meanwhile Venn and Thomasin approach the scene, encumbered by the baby, whose name, Eustacia Clementine Wildeve, ironically perpetuates the fatal triangle. Venn, the fallible local providence, by failing to stop the weeping Eustacia (whom he had glimpsed as she had unknowingly passed his van on her descent from Rainbarrow) has already missed one chance to prevent the catastrophe; and now he arrives too late to save anyone but Clym, who wishes only to die.

Again, the structure of the action in this climactic scene has under-girdings of symbolism and ritual. Clym and Wildeve follow Eustacia into the torrent in the order and manner in which they have fallen in love with her; and, as they have been whirled and driven by their passions, the three struggling lovers now revolve helplessly in the whirlpool. Venn pulls Clym out only after a grim tug of war with the corpse of Wildeve, whose arms are locked round Clym's legs. Apart from its symbolism, this last detail suggests a final struggle in the water between Clym and his rival – or, at least, an attempt by Wildeve to take Clym to the bottom with him. Another symmetry may also be noted in this scene. Just as the action of Book I begins with Venn leading the van in which Thomasin lies asleep, the action of Book V virtually ends with Venn supporting Thomasin on his arm and leading the cart which bears to the Quiet Woman the unconscious Clym and the corpses of Eustacia and Wildeve. The book closes with the final, ironic assembly of the fatal triangle, as the deathly Clym conducts Venn and Charley to view the lifelike bodies of the lovers in a room at the inn.

Book VI

As suggested by its title – 'Aftercourses' – and its brevity – only four short chapters – Book VI functions as an epilogue while winding up the post-catastrophic action. In fact, it was a Victorian convention, in both popular and classic fiction, to conclude with an epilogue in which any unsettled plot details could be disposed of and the devoted reader grat-ified with a glimpse of the 'aftercourses' of the story. However, Hardy's Book VI also evinces further development of plot and fulfilment of thematic anticipation, though critics have charged that this book violates the thematic unity of the novel as a whole.

Book VI opens on May Eve, eighteen months after the deaths of Eustacia and Wildeve, Chapter 1 establishing a gentler mood than the stormy ending of Book V. Book VI effectively begins with another 'return', the unexpected reappearance at Blooms-End of Venn, who has apparently not been seen since the catastrophe. This is Venn's fourth dramatic return to Egdon, counting his various reappearances, the first of which occurs at the very beginning of the novel when he takes Thomasin home in his van; the second on the evening when Wildeve intercepts the guineas; and the third on the day before Clym's 'discovery'. As Clym has resigned from the diamond business, Venn, on his humbler level, has now given up the disreputable but profitable trade in reddle; and he appears before the startled Thomasin and the astonished Clym as a respectable farmer, his face restored to the 'hues of an ordinary Christian countenance' (VI:i). The former reddleman, it is soon apparent, is now manoeuvring to win for himself the heath 'dimant' (diamond) – Fairway's epithet for Thomasin (I:v) – overlooked by Clym. Venn, always catalystic in the novel, soon reawakens the young widow's sexual feelings. But Clym is characteristically blind to Venn's manoeuvres, taking Thomasin's renewed bloom as a tribute to himself.

However, this new triangle remains tentative. Though 'it was even with a pleasant sense of doing his duty' (VI:iii) and deferring to his mother's longstanding wish that Clym prepares to marry his 'sweet cousin', he is relieved to find that her reawakening is owing to another man. At the same time, Clym obviously feels shock and regret when his proposal is forestalled by Thomasin's announcement that she wishes to accept Venn and will marry no one else. Clym instinctively voices his mother's supposed objection on social grounds to Venn, but he does not press the objection nor does he rise to Humphrey's suggestion later that he could still cut out Venn. Indeed, Clym seems to have been purged of all vehemence, reduced to 'the mere corpse of a lover' (VI:iii), by the weir-pool. While Venn's vitality irresistibly overcomes Thomasin's scruples against marrying a former reddleman, Clym is now clearly more at home with the dead, visiting the widely separated graves of his loved ones – his mother's by day and Eustacia's at night – in the intervals of his 'self-preparation' to become 'an itinerant preacher of the eleventh commandment' (VI:iii). Clym's gloomy satisfaction in his exclusion from life is graphically portrayed in the last scene at the significantly named Blooms-End, that of the wedding party of Thomasin and Venn. Clym deliberately remains outside the house, in company with his fellow melancholiac Charley, almost savouring his separation from the gaiety within. On the Sunday immediately following the wedding, Clym, again indulging in masochistic remorse, inaugurates his 'Sermons on the Mount' with a discourse apparently drawn from Solomon's brutal disappointment of his mother Bathsheba. Thus the novel closes with a parting of the ways between, on the one hand, Thomasin and Venn, who represent the renewal of life – as symbolized in their association with the Maypole – and, on the other, Clym, who represents nostalgia and regret, as symbolized by his grave-pulpit, Rainbarrow.

Book VI has frequently been criticized as anticlimactic as well as inconsistent in characterization, theme and tone with the first five books. In particular, Venn's reappearance in the character of a prosperous dairyman boasting a 'grand relative' in Budmouth has struck many critics as incongruous; and his coy assurance as a lover and antics as a bridegroom may seem to be consistent with neither his earlier character nor the generally sombre mood of the novel. Hardy himself invited such criticisms by revealing, in his footnote at the end of Chapter 3, that he had not originally intended Venn's final return and joyous union with Thomasin, this radical change in the ending having been forced upon him, as we know, by 'certain circumstances of serial publication'. But though various critics profess to be astonished by Hardy's admission, it must be kept in mind that changed or alternative endings were not uncommon in Victorian fiction. Dickens, for example, was persuaded by Bulwer-Lytton to change the ending of *Great Expectations* so that Pip could be united with Estella after all; and Charlotte Brontë, in order to humour her father, rewrote the unhappy ending of *Villette* (1853) in such a way as to allow the reader the possibility of a happy ending.

In *The Return*, notwithstanding certain inconsistencies that may be detected in Book VI — Venn's 'grand relative' is surely a false note — Hardy was generally able, as our analysis has shown, to assimilate the 'happy ending', to integrate this last book into the already established structure of action and theme. Even Venn's final transformation into a substantial citizen in bottle-green coat and blue-spotted neckerchief is foreshadowed in Chapter 7 of Book II, in which the reddleman dons respectable clothes in a quickly abandoned attempt to renew his addresses to Thomasin. Moreover, Venn's final return in triumph, through its reflection on the failure of Clym's return, adds another ironic symmetry to the plot. In any event, Hardy gets his own back at last by juxtaposing the frolic of the wedding with the irremediable sorrow of Clym, who attends in the shadows outside Blooms-End (where Eustacia had once listened to the merriment of the Christmas party), while inside the role of 'the skull at the banquet' (VI:iv) is filled by Christian. All in all, Book VI communicates an elegiac mood of completion, of our having come full circle. As Book I begins with Venn's bearing Thomasin in his hearse-like van to Blooms-End, Book VI concludes with his carrying her off from there, in a festive dogcart, to the marriage-bed. And the novel closes with the lone figure of Clym on Rainbarrow, where Eustacia had stood forlornly at the beginning.

Thematic Unity

Let us now briefly review unity of action in *The Return* as a whole. We may first of all distinguish between main plot, which centres on Clym and Eustacia, and sub-plot, which is essentially about Venn and Thomasin. Main plot and sub-plot are alike dominated by the theme of life frustrated by adversity and misfortune, a theme which is most strikingly articulated by Eustacia in her final despair: 'I was capable of much; but I have been injured and blighted and crushed by things beyond my control!' (V:vii). This dominant theme is also evinced by the disastrous sexual and marital mismatches promoted by Hap. In its happy ending, which is still not reached without much suffering, the sub-plot functions as an ironic comment on the main plot. Venn's triumph in Book VI sharpens our sense of the triumph of circumstances or the 'coil of things' over Clym, Eustacia, Wildeve and Mrs Yeobright. Fate is certainly the antagonist; even conflict between rivals in the various triangles is nothing to the ultimate conflict between each character and destiny. The characters who come off best – Venn and Thomasin – are those who least challenge destiny; who are most at home with their natural environment.

Three implicit structural devices undergird narrative coherence and focus the theme of fatality. The first and most obvious of these devices is simple coincidence, to which we shall return in a moment; the second is correspondence of event and place; and the third is chronological symmetry. The second device is evident, to take the central example, in the recurrence of action on Rainbarrow. That site of irony sees Eustacia's opening appearance as 'queen of the solitude' (I:ii) as well as her final breakdown as hopeless 'captive'; it sees Clym's induction into sexual passion, in the plighting of his troth to Eustacia, as well as his debut as a preacher of brotherly love. Another ominous spot is the pool at Mistover Knap. Here Eustacia and Wildeve have their first and last meetings; and the latter's figurative presence haunts the two other fatal meetings here, namely the *tête-à-tête* of Clym and Eustacia in the well-bucket scene and Eustacia's 'rencounter' with her mother-in-law.

Action is also generally unified by chronological symmetry, i.e. the structuring of narrative upon seasonal and calendar progression. Without using extended flashbacks or otherwise disarranging chronological sequence, Hardy induces a sense of *déjà vu* through the cyclic nature of his time-scheme as well as through repetitive correspondence of event and place. Verisimilitude in the passage of time is largely achieved through this implicit seasonal parallel of engendering, growth and fulfilment, as the plot unfolds through the traditional narrative cycle of a year and a day. Thus we have the beginning of the action on Guy Fawkes Day, the first meeting of Clym and Eustacia on Christmas Day, the wedding of Thomasin and Wildeve shortly after New Year's Day, the pledging of troths by Clym and Eustacia around the Ides of March (the midpoint of the novel), their wedding around Midsummer Day (24 June), the death of Clym's mother in the heat of the last day of August, the casting off of Eustacia and the birth of Thomasin's daughter around Michaelmas (29 September), and finally the recurrence of Guy Fawkes Day. In Book VI Thomasin is reawakened by Venn on May Eve a year and a half after the catastrophe.

However, of all the implicit structural devices in *The Return*, unlucky coincidence or the concatenation of such coincidences is the one most implicating fatality. If Christian had not been sidetracked to the raffle, Mrs Yeobright's guineas would not have been misdirected. If Eustacia had not chanced to meet Wildeve at the 'gipsying', or if he had not subsequently appeared at Alderworth just before Mrs Yeobright's arrival, or if Clym had not then cried out 'Mother' in his sleep, Mrs Yeobright would not have died on the heath. Again, if Clym had not put off for one day sending his letter to Eustacia, or if Fairway had delivered it a few hours earlier, Eustacia would not have died that night. Such aleatory links in the chain of causation have led critics to question the plausibility of Hardy's plot. In reply to this criticism, we may observe that Hardy so interweaves irony of incident in his narrative fabric that there is little feeling of disbelief in meeting coincidences; only when they are abstracted from narrative context and examined as independent possibilities do Hardy's coincidences seem implausible.

Criticism of Hardy's reliance on the convention of coincidence often implies that his catastrophes are *caused* by coincidence. But in *The Return* coincidence is not itself a cause; it is, rather, a variable detail in a pattern of events, a pattern ultimately revealed as fatality. If Mrs Yeobright's guineas had not gone astray, some other cause of mortal quarrel between her and Eustacia would surely have arisen, given their respective temperaments and the circumstances. If Eustacia had not met Wildeve at the 'gipsying', some other occasion would have brought them together again, given their respective yearnings and their past. The coincidence itself merely focuses the fatality immanent in the underlying 'coil of things'. This is the point Hardy was apparently making when, in his last revision of *The Return*, he qualified the account of Eustacia's flight by inserting the sentence, 'Even the receipt of Clym's letter would not have stopped her now' (V:vii). And even if Eustacia had received the letter in good time, how lasting would the reconciliation have been? How long could Eustacia have endured life at Blooms-End after it had become a shrine to the memory of Clym's mother?

For Hardy, then, coincidence is a conjunction of event, character and fate. As a structural device, it undergirds the analogical design of his plot. Just as Dickens's coincidences reveal the moral design of the universe, coincidence in *The Return* implicates an ultimate amorality, if not the outright malignity of destiny. But with this transformation of the naturalistic theme of adverse circumstances, with this personification of fate, we reach the limits of the realistic plot.

Characterization in the Realistic Plot

We move on now to the element of character and its interaction with plot in *The Return*. Here too the theme of fatality is apparently dominant. In Hardy's 'Novels of Character and Environment', character is evidently foredoomed to defeat, as are Clym and Eustacia in their respective struggles against 'that waggery of fate' (III:i) which has misplaced them. But this fatality is manifest not only in external adversity, in the circumstances which hem in life; it is also within character, working through the predispositions and other innate forces which play their part in the frustration of intention and aspiration. Although Hardy does not seem to have encountered Novalis's dictum, 'Character is Fate', until he had begun *The Mayor of Casterbridge*, this dictum is practically illustrated in the demiurges of heredity and environment which have shaped and indelibly marked character in *The Return*. Venn does finally wash off his reddle; but Clym, Eustacia, Mrs Yeobright and Wildeve never change their spots. Clym's native instincts rise again and again to frustrate his intentions; Eustacia is a prisoner of her past as much as of the heath; Mrs Yeobright, the curate's daughter long isolated among the heathfolk, has hardened in the mould of convention; Wildeve, to his own and others' detriment, naturally lacks a 'strong puritanic force within him' (IV:vi).

However, when we look at the actual interface of plot and character, i.e. motivation, we find not only determinism, but also a pervasive ambiguity in the action, a recurrent blurring of distinction between predetermination and intention. In *The Return*, as in Hardy's other 'Novels of Character and Environment', decisive movements in plot arise from some action which is determined, in turn, by the whole nature and total antecedents of a character. Wildeve's jilting of Eustacia, Clym's return and Eustacia's offering herself to Clym are three such actions. But once set in motion, the train of events develops an independent momentum; this spontaneity of purpose is strikingly illustrated in Charley's innocent kindling of the bonfire that summons Wildeve to his last tryst with Eustacia. On the other hand, coincidences, mishaps, and oversights often seem to express the unfulfilled intentions and subconscious urges of characters. When Mrs Yeobright seeks out Eustacia at Mistover, she does not *intend* to quarrel; but the guineas so dominate her thoughts that she fails to realize how insulting her enquiry about them sounds. At the same time, Mrs Yeobright is unconsciously spoiling for a fight with her 'supplanter'.

Indeed, Hardy anticipates Freud's contention that there are no accidents. Wildeve's 'error' with the licence, together with the 'coincidence' of his fixing Guy Fawkes Day as the wedding day, echoes his split between Thomasin and Eustacia. Similarly, Eustacia's burning of her hand on the well rope seems to express an unconscious response to Clym's interest in her as a 'martyr', if not her own latent urge to self-destruction. It is in the context of this general ambiguity of action and intention that we may also see the problem of Eustacia's end. Her previous attempt – frustrated by Charley – to shoot herself as well as her final despair leads us to infer that her death is suicide. Moreover, it has been pointed out that according to Hardy's map Eustacia could not have reached the weir without crossing the road on which Wildeve was waiting with his gig; she must, then, have finally preferred the weir to him. Nevertheless, at the time of her death, she is apparently in the grip of a despair and desperation having the effect of the compulsion symbolized by Susan's spell. In taking her own life, Eustacia might be seen as exhibiting the same 'diminished responsibility' as that adjudged in the case of Boldwood's murder of Troy in *Far from the Madding Crowd*. If, on the other hand, she did *fall* into the weir – notwithstanding her knowledge of the heath and despite the road clearly separating the heath from the weir in the meads – this 'accident' fulfils her repeatedly expressed expectation of and desire for death. Acquiescence in disaster may be seen even in Mrs Yeobright's death; Clym had often warned her not to cross the heath in the heat of summer.

However, despite the ambiguity which shadows their actions and intentions, despite the impersonal forces which mould and manipulate them, Hardy's characters do not, on the whole, strike us as puppets. They suffer too intensely, as beings bitterly or pathetically conscious of 'crass Casualty' and universal injustice, to be denied full dignity as personalities. Eustacia's final cry, 'O, how hard it is of Heaven to devise such tortures for me, who have done no harm to Heaven at all!' (V:vii), may be determined, in realistic terms, by neurosis and selfishness; but it is nonetheless moving. Nor can free will appear to be totally absent when poignant self-consciousness is retained. Even as the pattern of fatality enmeshes them, Hardy's characters retain the detachment to perceive that pattern. Thus Eustacia, amazed at the spontaneous combustion of her bonfire on the forgotten anniversary – and realizing whom 'that fire might call up' – 'could now ... take a standing-point outside herself, observe herself as a disinterested spectator, and think what a sport for Heaven this woman Eustacia was' (V:v).

Some critics, notably Roy Morrell, maintain that Hardy actually means to indict his characters for their passiveness, their failure to act responsibly in the face of catastrophe which is *not* inevitable. Support for this view appears in a notebook entry which Hardy made just as he was finishing *The Return*:

A Plot, or Tragedy, should arise from the gradual closing in of a situation that comes of ordinary human passions, prejudices, and ambitions, by reason of the characters taking no trouble to ward off the disastrous events produced by the said passions, prejudices, and ambitions.

We might see this failure to take effective action not only in Eustacia's habit of rationalization, but also in a certain acquiescence in fate which characterizes her, as it does Tess. Following the disaster of Mrs Yeobright's visit to Alderworth, Eustacia, instead of blaming herself, 'laid the fault upon the ... Prince of the World' (IV:viii). Moreover, on that same occasion Eustacia exhibits a habitual moral languor, an inclination to 'let events fall out as they might sooner than wrestle hard to direct them' (IV:vii). We might also see a culpable irresponsibility in the stubbornness, procrastination, and negligence which generally characterize the actions of Clym and his mother. Why did Mrs Yeobright entrust her guineas to a half-wit like Christian? Why did Clym put off reconciliation first with his mother and then his wife?

At the same time, however, there is an indeterminableness of responsibility and guilt in *The Return*, just as there is an ambiguity surrounding intention. When Clym demands to know whose fault the misunderstanding between Eustacia and his mother was, Eustacia replies, with some reason, that 'it was the fault of the circumstances' (IV:ii). And later, when Clym condemns himself as the cause of Eustacia's suicide, Venn replies, 'You may as well say that the parents be the cause of a murder by the child, for without the parents the child would never have been begot' (V:ix). Thus it is difficult to follow those critics who see an existentialist moral in the characters' failure to 'ward off' catastrophe in *The Return*. In Hardy's fiction, fate, not responsibility, is man's burden. Moreover, as we have already said, this fate is also within man, working through those all-too-human failings, those quirks, irrationalities and blindnesses which play their part in the chain of doom. Intention and accident, will and compulsion, character and fate are alike inseparable.

Character Analyses

Let us now review Hardy's characterization. As we look briefly at each of the main characters, several points should be kept in mind. First, Hardy, unlike George Eliot and James, makes comparatively little use of direct psychological analysis. Apart from the set-piece descriptions of Clym and Eustacia, motivation and the inner life of characters in *The Return* are often implied by action or metaphor; thus Clym's moral blindness is suggested by the impairment of his sight, and his mother fixation is emphasized by the allusion to Oedipus. The second point is that Hardy's delineation of character, in keeping with the other ironies of structure, is ironic in its pattern of implication. This basic pattern of irony is illustrated again by Clym's blindness or even by his name, if we think of his *inclemency* towards Eustacia. Third, we have in Hardy's characters a paradoxical duality, a 'bifocal' view, as Ian Gregor and others have noted. Clym, it might be argued, is on the one hand a rebel and a saint, and on the other a mamma's boy and a prig; Eustacia is simultaneously a deeply moving personage and a bandmaster's daughter who has read too much Byron; Wildeve is both sentimentalist and cynic. Finally, we may note that in *The Return* characters do not so much develop as exhibit the working out of preordained patterns.

We begin our character reviews with Clym, who is a study in inner conflict and self-division. Ironically, in yielding to the pull of nostalgia, renouncing worldly ambition, and returning to his beloved heath, Clym has not only challenged fate, but has also precipitated conflict with his own roots. His dedication to revolutionary social ideals must necessarily conflict with the unchanging traditions and mores of the heath, which are, moreover, instinctive in himself and implicit in his yeoman ancestry. This conflict is externalized in the opposition to his return voiced by his mother, his virtual alter ego, who personifies an ambition, pride and unyielding will which are inherent too in Clym. The self-division implicit in Clym's attraction to the antithetical Eustacia is twofold. His passion for her physical splendour is incompatible with his philanthropic project and ultimately with his instinctive austerity. More agonizingly, however, Clym's bond to his mother makes him ashamed of his sexual passion. While Eustacia's first kiss 'lingered upon his lips like a seal set there', Clym 'hardly dared to enter the house, for it seemed as if his mother might say, "What red spot is that glowing upon your mouth so vividly?"'(III:iii). Indeed, though drawn with pre-Freudian unconsciousness, Clym is a psychologically exact picture of an Oedipal personality; and this profoundest of the ironies of Clym's self-division underlies his nostalgia, his marital troubles, his cycle of anxiety and depression, and his narcissism, a quality later associated by Freud with maternal rejection.

Following from Clym's self-division, narcissism or self-absorption is another organizing theme in his characterization. Narcissism may be inferred from his habitual introspection as well as from his tendency to see others as reflections of himself. The latter tendency seems to condition even his falling in love with Eustacia, whom he persists in seeing as another aspirant to the teaching profession. He seems to see her also as a native spirit of the heath who is yet 'above' it by virtue of education and outside perspective; in short, he loves in her a female Clym. Narcissism is also implicit in the mirror imagery associated with Clym as in the eclipse scene on Rainbarrow or the confrontation scene in Eustacia's bedroom. In the latter scene there is an uncanny effect of self-projection; we see both faces in the glass while the 'carmine flush' fades from Eustacia's face and 'the death-like pallor in his face flew across into hers' (V:iii), reflecting Clym's transference of blame in his mother's death. In addition to mirrors, Clym, as suggested also by his surname, is associated with other shining objects like diamonds, the moon and lamps. We repeatedly see Clym glowing in firelight or moonlight; we also see him with his reading lamp and oil as he prepares to enlighten Egdon. Yet, not only is the light-bearer himself soon afflicted by darkness, but already in the mumming scene Clym's worn face shows that 'mental luminousness must be fed with the oil of life' (II:vi). The latter metaphor recurs during Clym's delirium after his mother's death, when he is 'consuming himself by the gnawing of his thought', and 'his eyes [are] lit by a hot light, as if the fire in their pupils were burning up their substance' (V:i). Thus Clym is finally self-consuming as well as self-absorbed; he is burnt out by his own brilliance as well as by his egoistic assumption of guilt.

In writing of the ironies of Clym's return and the dilemma of his relations with his mother, Hardy was working with a sureness of insight drawn, perhaps not always consciously, from his own deepest feelings. However, as a representative of 'modern' thought and an apostle of the eleventh commandment, Clym seems less convincing, though self-appointed preachers were no anomaly in the age of Carlyle and Ruskin. Various critics have observed that Clym's final depletion of vitality seems to affect also his verisimilitude as a character; that he is in danger, especially in Book VI, of fading into a mere abstraction. Though we must not take Clym's weakness in character for Hardy's weakness in characterization, there are various inconsistencies and a seepage of vagueness in Clym's role as a thinker, an idealist, and even a native. We too often hear of Clym's identity past and present with the heath, instead of seeing that identity embodied. In Book VI we wonder what has become of his social philosophy. We may also wonder how so impractical a man could have managed a diamond business. Although Clym remains a compelling figure in his nostalgia and pathos, his characterization is perhaps the least resolved of all Hardy's protagonists.

In contrast, Mrs Yeobright is one of Hardy's most convincing characters. She is dominated, in the first place, by the fierce respectability of the minor gentry; hence her sternness with Thomasin, her distrust of Eustacia and Wildeve, her coolness towards Venn, and her aloofness from the heath-folk. The objects associated with her, namely house plants and the heirloom guineas, are emblematic, respectively, of domesticity and thrift. Her uncompromising uprightness is the obvious source of her son's earnestness, just as the self-pity in which she later indulges – 'I am only a poor old woman who has lost a son' (IV:i) – is the complement of his narcissism. No hypocrite, she is unaware of the jealousy underlying her moralistic disapproval of Eustacia, whom she finds 'a voluptuous, idle woman' (III:v). Indeed, this irrational level of her motivation is generally unconscious in the novel. She is infuriated by Clym's 'indiscretion' in speaking of his beloved with 'fervour'; but the narrator assures us that 'Hardly a maternal heart within the four seas could . . . have helped being irritated at that ill-timed betrayal of feeling for a new woman' (III:iii). Thus Mrs Yeobright is portrayed not as a type of abnormality, but rather as a type of maternity. However, Hardy indicates the disastrous effects of this vehement maternity; like the sexual instinct, it forms part of the fatal order of things trapping Clym. It is also her own destruction. Just as Clym is agonized by her anger, she is driven back upon the heath by what she takes to be his rejection of her.

The remaining Yeobright, Thomasin, shows the family qualities in her domesticity and maternity as well as in her filial regard for both her aunt and the heath. On the other hand, though she prefers Wildeve to Venn, she generally shows a common sense and a simple charity quite uncharacteristic of the Yeobrights. Of all Hardy's heroines, Thomasin is perhaps the gentlest and least capricious, though she does not lack the family spirit. She replies 'vehemently' to her aunt's rebuke: 'Now, look at me as I kneel here, picking up these apples – do I look like a lost woman? . . . I wish all good women were as good as I!' (II:ii). Hardy informed his illustrator that Thomasin was to be pictured as the 'good' heroine in contrast to Eustacia; and we repeatedly see this opposition in Hardy's own portrayal. While Eustacia is a figure of night, Thomasin is 'illuminated' by an 'oblique band of sunlight . . . as her presence illuminated the heath' (III:vi). We also see Thomasin transfigured by sunlight as she chooses apples in the loft, pigeons fluttering about her head. Other auspicious symbols cluster about her, not least the Maypole. Gathering holly, she is garlanded by this ancient sign of fertility; and in a quartet of similes she is likened to the kestrel, the heron, the kingfisher and the swallow, all birds of good omen.

We move on now to Eustacia. In the first place, we have in her thematic opposition to Thomasin the Victorian convention of pairing a dark heroine and a fair one, the dark one being in some way mysterious, tainted or dangerous, and all the more attractive for being so. Hence Eustacia's audacity, passion, and Mediterranean blood as well as her 'magic reputation': 'Good girls don't get treated as witches even on Egdon' (III:ii). However, Hardy has enriched this convention almost beyond recognition and transformed it into a major structural pattern. Even a detail like the holly in Thomasin's hair is countered by the 'prickly tuft' of furze entangled in Eustacia's hair, like a hint of a crown of thorns. Eustacia's 'shady splendour' contrasts with Thomasin's illumination and seems to obscure Clym's radiance, like the shadow eclipsing the moon above their tryst on Rainbarrow. While 'the sun . . . made a mirror of Thomasin's [braided] hair' (II:viii), Eustacia's unbound hair is 'like nightfall extinguishing the western glow' (I:vii). Eustacia is also associated with fire – we see her waving a flaming bough – but the implication is of a blaze followed by eternal extinction. While Thomasin receives golden coins, Eustacia is given a cremation urn; but her chosen emblems are the telescope and the hourglass, symbols, respectively, of longing and death.

Thus, in contrast to Thomasin's association with the renewal of life, the omens and tokens attracted by Eustacia suggest a morbid discontent verging on self-destructiveness. This morbidity is suggested also in her masochism, her 'courting' of her 'own discomfiture by love' (II:vi). Moreover, Eustacia totally lacks Thomasin's filial character; and she hates not only the heath but also, as she declares to Clym, Mother Nature. In this way Eustacia's hatred of the heath is linked with her hostility towards her mother-in-law. The 'absolute queen' of her indulgent grandfather's household, Eustacia is Electra to Clym's Oedipus; and her repudiation of the mother is as ominous as Clym's overdependence. Ironically, Eustacia and her mother-in-law share much in temperament and will, both suffering from a 'stifled warmth' within; both 'forswearing compromise'; both opposing Clym's sacrifice of his career.

Eustacia's ironic self-division is also revealed in her obsession with the heath. Though loathing the heath as a prison, Eustacia owes to it her dignity: 'Isolation on a heath renders vulgarity well-nigh impossible . . . A narrow life in Budmouth might have completely demeaned her . . . In the captain's cottage she could suggest mansions she had never seen' (I:vii). Moreover, though 'Budmouth was her native place', Eustacia is, as she tells Wildeve, a 'denizen' of the heath (where, as the Postscript tells us, the name 'Eustacia' itself is indigenous). She has 'imbibed much of what was dark in its tone'; and she appears to be its very incarnation, so that Clym has some excuse for mistaking her. In mortally opposing the heath, Eustacia is not only deluding herself with the belief that life would be better elsewhere, but also repudiating a large part of her own being.

Critics have charged that Hardy fails to reconcile a central duality in Eustacia of neurotic daydreamer and grand rebel. However, it is in this duality or double perspective that we see the intersection of the realistic and tragic plots. Eustacia's demand for splendour, the grandeur of her naiveté, lifts her above the pettiness of the Budmouth milieu that produced her, the vision of gold-braided officers promenading on the esplanade that apparently inspires her.

We come next to Damon Wildeve, who, in his loathing of the heath, unfilial attitude towards Mrs Yeobright and Byronic aura, is a lesser counterpart of Eustacia. But though he assumes an outsider's sophistication, Wildeve is actually of local origin. Like Clym, he had been given a start in a professional career at Budmouth; but he has returned in failure to Egdon. Thus there is duality in Wildeve also, that of insolent defiance and bourgeois aspiration. However, of all the characters Wildeve is the closest to a stock character; like Manston and Alec d'Urberville, he is adapted from the seducer or 'spoiler'. This two-dimensional design persists in his description:

The grace of his movement was singular: it was the pantomimic expression of a lady-killing career. Next came into notice . . . a profuse crop of hair impending over the top of his face, lending to his forehead the high-cornered outline of an early Gothic shield; and a neck which was smooth and round as a cylinder.

(I:v)

He could treat a woman 'with such unparalleled grace as to make . . . the ruin of her honour [appear] as excess of chivalry' (IV:viii), and he panders to Eustacia's discontent: 'Such a rare plant in such a wild place it grieves me to see' (V:v). 'Cursed with sensitiveness, and blue demons' (I:v), Wildeve is also a man of feeling, 'the Rousseau of Egdon' (IV:vi); but – again typically – his sentiment is underlaid by a streak of cruelty. Thomasin, while herself suffering from Wildeve's caprice, congratulates him on being unable to 'bear the sight of pain in even an insect' (I:v); and, with precise irony, we later see him pricking glow-worms and burning a moth. Yet he is far from being simply a villain. Like the moth, he cannot resist Eustacia's fire; his saving grace is his impulsiveness, which often works against his own interests, so that his final plunge is consistent with his character. Again consistently, Wildeve is a gambler not only at dice, but in the ironic lottery of fate. He loses at engineering, wins Thomasin, loses Eustacia, wins a fortune, and loses his life. Finally we see the symbolic banknotes drying by the fire as their erstwhile owner grows cold.

In Venn, the last of the main characters, we have the duality of 'Ishmaelitish' wanderer and respectable yeoman. Indeed, Venn makes so convincing a reddleman that his final return to landholding is almost disappointing. Reddle, which is, after all, merely a dye made from clay, becomes on Venn a paradoxical mixture of the mundane and the uncanny; a stigma, but also a sign of natural vitality, like the Maypole with which he is also associated. But from the beginning Venn's grotesquery is offset by evidences of a humane and even kindly disposition. On the other hand, in keeping with his role of outcast, Venn also shows a disposition to take the law into his own hands as well as a talent at spying which has struck some readers as voyeurism. Others have found Venn's assumption of the role of local providence unconvincing, though this role is consistent with other aspects of his character. In his shrewdness, tenacity and faithfulness, Venn, like Gabriel Oak, is an idealized yeoman. Like Clym, Venn is also identified with the heath (his name means *fen*); but Venn draws resolution and steadfastness from his natural environment. His tenacity is like that of the heather which cultivation cannot eradicate; like the heath itself, he is 'slighted and enduring' (I:i). The filial relationship which he develops with Mrs Yeobright is another parallel with Clym; and we finally see Venn not only as a foil to Wildeve, but also as an ironic counterpart of Clym.

Setting and Realism in *The Return of the Native*

It is in setting that the simultaneity of the realistic and the nonrealistic in *The Return* is most apparent. Of course, Egdon Heath, whether taken as an actual south-Dorset heath or as a metaphoric wasteland, is one of the most remarkable aspects of the novel. The opening evocation of the heath establishes an atmosphere that hardly lifts even in Book VI; and none of the subsequent description or action is free of that darkling presence, which bends both character and the trajectory of plot. In the heath the element of setting seems to impinge upon the functions of other elements; hence the common remark that the heath itself is the protagonist. However, for the moment, let us put the heath back into perspective as a literal place and but one component of setting, in order to look at the realistic aspect of Hardy's setting.

In its greatest geographical extent this setting is Wessex, Hardy's name, 'disinterred' from the West Saxon kingdom of the Heptarchy, for the five or six counties roughly comprising the West Country. As Hardy explained in the Preface to the Wessex Edition of *Far from the Madding Crowd*, the novel in which Wessex is first named, 'The series of novels I projected being mainly of the kind called local, they seemed to require a territorial definition of some sort to lend unity to their scene.' Needless to say, Hardy's Wessex, like its descendant, Faulkner's Yoknapatawpha County, is one of the great triumphs of regionalism in the novel. It is perhaps less well appreciated that Wessex is the culmination of a 'local' tradition in the British novel going back, through Scott, at least to the West-Country setting of *Tom Jones*. Hardy's immediate inspiration in modelling a fictional world upon a 'real' province of England was probably Trollope's 'Barsetshire' series, notably *Barchester Towers* (1857), 'Barchester' being an amalgam of Winchester and Salisbury. However, Hardy was also attracted by the historical aspect of regionalism, with its emphasis (as in Scott) on wild landscape and folk tradition, though only one of Hardy's own novels, *The Trumpet-Major*, is historical. We have already noted the formative influence in *The Return* of Ainsworth's *Lancashire Witches: A Romance of Pendle Forest*; and Hardy also admired Blackmore's *Lorna Doone: A Romance of Exmoor* (1869), which incorporates Monmouth's Rebellion in its setting.

Yet *The Return* was not subtitled *A Romance of Egdon Heath*; as shown by Trollope's 'Barset', it was realism, not romance, which was at the heart of regionalism. After reading *Lorna Doone* in 1875, Hardy wrote to Blackmore, as one West Countryman to another, praising his precise observation of nature. Hardy set out his own concern 'to preserve . . . a fairly true record of a vanishing life', in his General Preface to the Wessex Edition, the edition which finally shaped each novel to a definite time and place in the Wessex scheme: 'At the dates represented in the various narrations things were like that in Wessex: the inhabitants lived in certain ways, engaged in certain occupations, kept alive certain customs, just as they are shown doing in these pages.' But realism was implicit in regionalism not only in the painstaking fidelity to landscape, dialect, folklore, or mores, but also in the characteristic interrelationship of native and locality. In its typical derivation of character from environment, the regional novel directly applied the determinism underlying nineteenth-century realism. This takes us back yet again to Hardy's label, 'Novels of Character and Environment', and to Clym's relation to the heath: 'He was permeated with its scenes, with its substance, and with its odours. He might be said to be its product' (III:ii).

The Return presents an accurate picture of one corner of provincial life. As Hardy tells us in his Preface, the time is the 1840s, a dating confirmed by Charley's willingness to be transported for Eustacia's sake, since transportation was virtually abolished in 1850. The time, then, is that of Hardy's childhood; and the ambience of remoteness and isolation reflects that of Higher Bockhampton before the extension of the railway to Dorchester. The social setting of the novel is confined to the minor 'gentility' – the 'gig-gentry', as they are called in *Far from the Madding Crowd* – of the Dorset heath villages who occupy a transitional phase between the old yeoman class and the new professional middle class. Indeed, no other Wessex novel is more circumscribed both geographically and socially; only *Under the Greenwood Tree* and *The Woodlanders* are at all comparable in restriction of scale. But the people making up this Egdon society are neither the conventional provincials of Trollope and Eliot nor the 'shabby-genteel' class of Thackeray and Dickens; still less are they the petty bourgeoisie of *Madame Bovary*. Hardy's provincials such as the Yeobrights are individualized by a naiveté, stubbornness, and even crustiness ill-suited to their middle-class propriety; but, above all, they are distinguished by an indigenousness transcending social class. Like their servants, the heath-folk, they are rooted in the land; conjoined with the countryside in a web of association, memory and tradition. 'Clym had been so interwoven with the heath in his boyhood that hardly anybody could look upon it without thinking of him' (III:i). To be a native, according to *The Woodlanders*, is to

know all about those invisible ones of the days gone by ... [to] recall whose creaking plough has turned those sods from time to time; whose hands planted the trees that form a crest to the opposite hill; whose horses and hounds have torn through that underwood; what birds affect that particular brake; what bygone domestic dramas of love, jealousy, revenge, or disappointment have been enacted in the cottages, the mansions, the street or on the green.

This nostalgic sense of pre-industrial nativeness is Hardy's unique contribution to regionalism, and such a contribution could probably have come only from an author whose origins lay outside the cultural centre of his society. Ultimately, Hardy's sense of place verges on the mystic; but it is always grounded in the concrete.

In *The Return* Hardy 'documents' his narrative by the compelling authenticity of detail. Thus we have the minutiae of reddle-dealing and furze-cutting, the sudden glimpses into the lives of the heath-folk. In his mastery of folk speech, Hardy stands with Shakespeare, Scott, and Dickens. The heath-folk's language is not only an accurate reflection of West-Country dialect; it is also an expression of the ironic humour and fatalism of the Wessex peasant. Thus Fairway expounds the misfortune of being 'a man of no moon':

'No moon, no man.' 'Tis one of the truest sayings ever spit out. The boy never comes to anything that's born at new moon. A bad job for thee, Christian, that you should have showed your nose then of all days in the month.

(I:iii)

Hardy's use of folklore also reflects faithfully the rhythms of local life. Especially convincing is the 'stolidity' of the Egdon mummers, who perform as if 'moved by an inner compulsion to say and do their allotted parts whether they will or no' (II:iv). Folklorists confirm this 'perfunctory' character of genuine folk ritual; and research has also shown that in parts of south Dorset the fertility customs and ambience of the midsummer fires were, in fact, displaced to Guy Fawkes Day, as implied in the impromptu ember-dancing that follows the bonfire on Rainbarrow. Finally, we have the same 'documentary' authenticity in natural detail; in the always clearly visualized landscape, weather, sky and heavenly bodies, all of which frame the action; in the startlingly 'real' animals, birds, trees, ferns and flowers with which human life is intertwined. Even ants, moths and glow-worms come into sharp focus, completing the effect of microcosm. This microcosm is nearly congruent with Egdon Heath, which is detailed in its topographic, ecological, economic and historical aspects. As the heath is the habitat of plants and animals, it is also the natural home of the heath-folk, who have immemorially subsisted on its austere produce – furze, turf, thorn roots and berries. The 'Egdon waste' is even documented by the Domesday Book, in which it appears as 'Bruaria' (I:i).

Yet it is also in the heath that we first realize Hardy's transcendence of realism. In this sinister image of Eustacia and Wildeve on the heath, for example, we have an almost surrealistic transformation of the environmental theme: 'Their black figures sank and disappeared from against the sky. They were as two horns which the sluggish heath had put forth from its crown, like a mollusc, and had now again drawn in' (I:ix). Eventually we recognize in the heath a duality like that in character; a simultaneity of 'Titanic form' and relatively small tract of wasteland. Indeed, many readers remember the heath as – and expect to find in Dorset – a literal wilderness like Dartmoor, though, in fact, Mrs Yeobright crosses and recrosses it in one afternoon. In short, in the heath we have the first indication of the 'bifocal' principle in setting. Refocusing on the Egdon community, we see, despite the meticulously authentic detail, something other than realism, something quite different from the complex socioeconomic analysis of Eliot's *A Study of Provincial Life*, as *Middlemarch* (1872) was subtitled. In Hardy's reduction of society to two or three households, we have a principle of minimalization that has little to do with realism. There is a similarly nonrealistic exclusion of the outside world; only two places outside Wessex are mentioned, namely Eustacia's vaguely conceived Paris and an even vaguer America, where Wildeve's kin live, the narrator even seeming to confuse Wisconsin and Canada. Within Wessex itself, the only place beyond Egdon which is pictured at all is Budmouth; and that former Georgian watering place appears only in Eustacia's rose-coloured reveries and Venn's slyly tantalizing vision of 'thousands of gentlepeople walking up and down – bands of music playing – officers by sea and officers by land walking among the rest' (I:x).

What we have ultimately, then, in *The Return* – and in no other Wessex novel – is a metaphoric isolation of setting and action that is comparable only to that of a novel like *Wuthering Heights*. Like Emily Brontë, though not with the same demonic characterization, Hardy creates a moral universe from the polarity of two isolated houses. Just as the sheltered Thrushcross Grange symbolically opposes Wuthering Heights, Blooms-End, surrounded by genteel white palings in its fertile valley, opposes the upland Mistover Knap, which is banked and ditched on its barren slopes like a Dark Age redoubt. Yet character in *The Return* finds its principal metaphor in the heath, as character in *Wuthering Heights* reflects the moor. The passionate interrelationship of all Hardy's characters and the heath is obvious, but the symbolism of the heath is constantly shifting. In keeping with the hatred and love which it inspires, the heath represents qualities or powers that are within man as well as those that are external and alien to him; it may diminish him or it may offer a vision of grandeur that trivializes even Paris. As we shall see presently, the heath is the indispensable frame to the tragic plot; and we may also think of it as the heart of Wessex, the central manifestation of Hardy's principle of setting, as stated in his General Preface, that 'that which is apparently local should be really universal'.

Point of View and Voice

In *The Return*, as in the other Wessex novels, we have an apparently conventional third-person narration, with an omniscient narrator privy to the characters' thoughts, though he does not always exercise this privilege. This narrator avails himself occasionally of the authorial first person plural – 'And so we have our Eustacia – for at times she was not altogether unlovable' (I:vii) – though he never uses the authorial 'I'. Like the typical narrator of the Victorian novel – and unlike the self-effacing, Jamesian narrator who is more common in the modern novel – Hardy's narrator might also be called intrusive, inasmuch as he interpolates comment or even discursive editorializing. For example, Venn's ascent of Mistover Knap to confront Eustacia inspires this reflection on the local birds:

Feathered species sojourned here in hiding which would have created wonder if found elsewhere. A bustard haunted the spot and not many years before this five and twenty might have been seen in Egdon at one time. Marsh-harriers looked up from the valley by Wildeve's. A cream-coloured courser had used to visit this hill, a bird so rare that not more than a dozen have ever been seen in England; but a barbarian rested neither night nor day till he had shot the African truant, and after that event cream-coloured coursers thought fit to enter Egdon no more.

(I:x)

In such a passage we feel the presence not only of the rural essayist, but also of an interpreter introducing outlandish scenes. This interpreter's voice, which is characteristic of regional fiction at least since Scott, is especially marked in Chapter 3 of Book I, entitled 'The Custom of the Country', though this mediating voice is a recurrent aspect of Hardy's intrusive narrator: 'But in upland hamlets the transition from a-bed to abroad is surprisingly swift and easy. There no dense partition of yawns and toilets divides humanity by night from humanity by day' (V:ii).

The language and tone of this narrator are also apparently the conventional ones of Victorian formality. The diction tends to be Latinate and polysyllabic: 'Feathered species sojourned here in hiding' rather than 'Kinds of birds hid here'. In his naturalist's tone the narrator even refers to furze as *Ulex Europaeus*. The syntax is similarly laboured, like a literal translation from Latin: 'Thus to deplore, each from his point of view, the mutually destructive interdependence of spirit and flesh would have been instinctive with these in critically observing Yeobright' (II:vi). The exposition is interspersed with conventional tropes, epigrams, rhetorical questions and exclamations: 'Fair prospects wed happily with fair times; but alas, if times be not fair!' (I:i). 'No style in literature, save Scott's,' Virginia Woolf observes, 'is so difficult to analyse; it is on the face of it so bad, yet it achieves its aim so unmistakably.' But perhaps we can get over this difficulty in analysis by treating style in *The Return* as another aspect of a deliberate projection, another element in fictional voice. Even as we recognize the formality of the narrator's speech, however, we must also acknowledge its idiosyncracy. It is sometimes lavish and eloquent – as in the 'Queen of Night' chapter – at other times gnarled and cragged like the heath. A simile like the following is peculiar in its vividness to Hardy's narrator: 'oozing lumps of fleshy fungi ... like the rotten liver and lungs of some colossal animal' (V:vii).

Indeed, the narrator in *The Return* is not Fielding's or Trollope's personal one, who genially takes the reader into his confidence. In *Barchester Towers*, for example, the narrator strolls onto the stage in order to assure 'the gentle-hearted reader' that Eleanor will not marry the odious Mr Slope. But the voice of Hardy's narrator, though intrusive and idiosyncratic, remains at the same time so anonymous and impersonal that critics have likened it to that of the saga or ballad. It is this grim, foreboding voice that opens and closes the novel; that invokes the spirit of the heath; that narrates the catastrophe. What we have, then, in *The Return* is a shifting voice which becomes, by turns, intrusive and impersonal, while the authorial presence – what Aristotle called the ethos – remains as elusive as that of God in post-Christian nature. This protean nature of voice is established in the Egdon Heath overture, in which the brooding voice of the *genius loci* is interspersed with the scenic observations of the Victorian traveller, as in the allusions to Heidelberg, Baden and 'the sand-dunes of Scheveningen'. Critics are undecided whether Hardy deliberately manipulates the convention of third-person narration or whether he is simply careless of his shifts, spoiling unity of tone for the sake of learned digressions. However, his conscious design here would be consistent with that principle of simultaneity which obtains in other aspects of structure in *The Return*.

Another striking singularity in Hardy's narrator – and one which certainly sets him apart from the narrator of realistic fiction – is the physical limitation in his purview. Virtually all the action that he narrates occurs within view of Rainbarrow, even events in nearby Anglebury appearing only in various secondhand reports. This concentration of perspective reinforces the isolation of setting. In the opening chapter we leave the outside world and move inward, with the narrator, along the white highway overlaying the Via Iceniana of the Romans and traversing the heath 'from one horizon to another'. Yet, beyond these narrowed horizons, we still glimpse 'the distant rims of the world and of the firmament' (I:i). In focusing inward the narrator does not relinquish his claims of universality.

Hardy's manipulation of perspective also involves a periodic shifting of point of view among the characters. This again contrasts with James's technique of unifying point of view in one character through whose consciousness we follow all events. In Chapters 9 and 10 of Book I, for example, following the narrator's discourse on reddlemen, we have a shift to the perspective of Venn, through whom we eavesdrop on Eustacia and Wildeve. When they move out of his earshot, we stay behind too. Similarly, in the mumming scene, we initially view Blooms-End and its inmates from the physical and psychological perspective of the spying Eustacia. The most complex example of espial appears in the discovery scene, in which we learn that Johnny Nunsuch saw Mrs Yeobright see Eustacia see her from the window; and while the unwitting child speaks, the horrified Clym 'sees' the incident mentally. The espial motif is reflected even in the 'keen round eyes' of birds, rabbits and reptiles who watch men; the heath itself at times 'became full of a watchful intentness' (I:i). Ultimately, we have the effect of a disembodied perspective or God's-eye view, as if we were looking through the wrong end of Eustacia's telescope. From this ironic perspective, Charley 'appeared on the dark ridge of heathland, like a fly on a negro' (II:iv); man diminishes, like Clym, to 'a brown spot in the midst of an expanse of olive-green gorse, and nothing more' (IV:ii).

Another of Hardy's techniques of perspective is the 'impression-picture' – his term in *The Woodlanders* – in which a character is frozen in a symbolic pose, or *tableau vivant*, as in the Victorian parlour game. This technique shows the influence not only of Rembrandt and Dutch genre painting, but also of contemporary narrative painting and photography. Typical *tableaux* in *The Return* are the lantern-lit view of Thomasin in the van ('Distressed Innocence Asleep'), Clym's chiaroscuro portrait ('The Introspective Man'), the candle-lit triptych of Clym, Fairway and Grandfer ('The Three Ages of Man'), and the final, *morbidezza* study of Eustacia ('Life in Death'). However, in addition to the time exposure focus of such *tableaux*, we also have 'cinematic' technique. In Chapter

113

6 of Book I, for example, our focus closes up, like a cinema camera in a night scene, upon the mysterious 'Figure against the Sky'. Details of Eustacia's form are intermittently lit up as we follow her from Rain-barrow to Mistover, and we glimpse her face only when she blows upon the embers. This experimentation with perspective and lighting is com-plemented by an almost obsessive recurrence of optical imagery; of mirrors, lenses, retinas and reflections. Certain scenes such as the gam-bling on the heath or Mrs Yeobright's arrival at Clym's cottage seem to take on the visual intensity of the diorama or of the camera obscura. Frequently, too, we have the effect of observed emotion recoiling, magnified, upon the observer, as when Eustacia sees Clym's face in her bedroom looking-glass, 'and the death-like pallor in his face flew across into hers' (V:iii). This shifting and refraction of perspective, like the shifting of voice, blurs the line between objectivity and subjectivity; and it reinforces the anonymity of the narrator and the principle of simultaneity.

The Tragic Level of Plot

We come now to tragic form in *The Return*, which, as we said, is 'dis-placed', i.e. submerged below the realistic surface of fictional form. This does not mean that Hardy's readers and reviewers were unaware of the tragic overtones, for by mid-Victorian times the idea of a 'tragic novel' was well established. Indeed, contemporary drama was so uninspired that the tragic muse seemed likely to emigrate to the novel. Accordingly, Bulwer-Lytton aspired to tragedy in his novel *Lucretia* (1846); and George Eliot in *Felix Holt* introduced a tragic theme of hereditary doom analogous to that plaguing Aeschylus's House of Atreus. Hardy finally acknowledged his own challenge of comparison with 'our magnificent heritage from the Greeks in dramatic literature', in his General Preface, in which he identified Wessex with Attica. In *The Return* the parallel with grand tragedy is hinted by allusions to Aeschylus, Sophocles, Shakespeare, Racine and Mrs Siddons as well as by other allusions such as the comparison of the misty Egdon hills to 'an archipelago in a fog-bound Aegean' (I:x). In the opening of the novel we are told that the heath 'had a lonely face, suggesting tragical possibilities'; but just before Clym's discovery it is Eustacia who has a 'tragic face' (V:i). Later we have a reference to a natural 'chorus' (III:vii), and in her last appearance Eustacia is said to 'soliloquize' (V:vii). However, Hardy intended not only to write a tragic novel, but also to create a simultaneity of forms; to write a novel which was itself a metaphor of tragedy. What we have, then, in *The Return* are not only tragic themes but also a simulation of tragic form.

Implicit tragic form in *The Return* includes, first of all, the division into five books (excluding the post-catastrophic Book VI), corresponding with the traditional five acts of tragedy, while the opening description of Egdon Heath and the short Book VI constitute, respectively, a prologue and an epilogue. Next we must mention again the figurative observance of the unities of time and place. Of course, the action, again excluding Book VI, is restricted in time to the cyclic year and a day. But it has been pointed out that this literal year becomes, in the narrator's metaphor, a 'day' on the heath, in keeping with the Aristotelian restriction:

> This flowering period [summer] represented the second or noontide division in the cycle of those superficial changes which alone were possible here; it followed the green or young fern period, representing the morn, and preceded the brown period, when the heath-bells and ferns would wear the russet tinges of evening; to be in turn displaced by the dark hue of the winter period, representing night.
>
> (IV:i)

Unity of place is realized in the restriction of action to the heath and its immediate vicinity, a *mise en scène* emphasized, in the first edition, by the map. Thus the heath becomes a metaphoric stage, and we have 'scenic' structure in the narrative. In the many set scenes there is typical stage business such as eavesdropping or the Shakespearean devices, in the mumming scene, of a girl disguised as a boy and a play within a play. Action often centres upon props such as the reddle van, or is framed by backdrops such as the pool at Mistover or the great barrow. As already mentioned, in some scenes we have an almost choreographic movement and grouping of characters as well as a symmetry of character, action and setting. Eustacia conceals herself from Wildeve in the van just as Thomasin had done; she quarrels with Mrs Yeobright at the pool, the site of her assignations with Wildeve. Hardy's scenes may have a formality of structure reminiscent of French classical tragedy, in which the entrance or exit of a character signals a change of scene. There are, moreover, theatrical overtones in the language of such scenes, a tendency for talk to take on the quality of speeches or stage dialogue. Hence the ripostes exchanged by Eustacia and Wildeve, the impassioned speeches in the confrontation between Clym and Eustacia, and Eustacia's final 'soliloquy'.

In fact, the best example of 'dramatic' structure in the novel, namely the confrontation scene in Eustacia's bedroom, which is the crisis of the action, is modelled upon Brachiano's reviling of Vittoria in Act IV,

Scene II, of Webster's tragedy, *The White Devil* (1612). In Hardy's scene the declamation and archaism ('Do you brave me? do you stand me out, mistress?') reflect the Jacobean model, while the prose sometimes paraphrases Webster's lines. Compare Clym's 'How bewitched I was! How could there be any good in a woman that everybody spoke ill of?' with Brachiano's

> I was bewitch'd;
> For all the world speaks ill of thee.

Moreover, in this scene the presence of the narrator is reduced to parentheses resembling stage directions. In such a scene we can see the novel form straining to transcend itself.

However, this scene also exemplifies the density of allusion, the thematic recapitulation of classic tragedy, which distinguishes *The Return*. Thus Clym's delirium of guilt following his mother's death recalls the Furies' torment of the matricidal protagonist of Aeschylus' *Oresteia* and Euripides' *Orestes*. Mrs Yeobright's appearance at the heath-folk's bonfire, in Chapter 3 of Book I, may deliberately echo the opening scene of the *Oresteia*, in which Clytemnestra speaks to the chorus while the beacon fires portend Agamemnon's return. Indeed, the adder which stings Mrs Yeobright also identifies her with Clytemnestra, who, according to Aeschylus, had dreamed that she bore a serpent, in whom she later recognized her son Orestes. (There is even an autobiographical reflection here in the story of the snake in Hardy's cradle.) On the other hand, Clym's ominous probing into the circumstances of his mother's death is reminiscent of Sophocles's Oedipus, who is mentioned at the moment of Clym's discovery. There are also Shakespearean echoes. Eustacia's consolation of Clym, 'Other men's mothers have died' (V:i), seems to recall the comfort offered to the grieving Hamlet by Gertrude and Claudius. Clym's murderous fury in the discovery that he has apparently been cuckolded – 'The strangest deeds were possible to his mood' (V:ii) – recalls Othello much more obviously than Webster's Brachiano. Moreover, Mrs Yeobright on the scorching heath, apparently cast off by her son and malignant daughter-in-law, seems to parallel Lear on his blasted heath – perhaps the very same heath, the Postscript reminds us. Lear's words certainly fit her death:

> How sharper than a serpent's tooth it is
> To have a thankless child!

Another structural parallel with grand tragedy in *The Return*, as one of its reviewers noted, is the implicit use of the heath-folk as a 'chorus'.

They assume this quasi-choral role on their first appearance, in which, in the intervals of the Guy Fawkes ritual, they comment on the doings of their betters and finally engage in dialogue with Mrs Yeobright. Unlike the classical chorus, however, Hardy's chorus consists of individualized members. It includes a *de facto* leader, Fairway, the furze dealer; the fool Grandfer Cantle and his 'maphrotight' son Christian; Sam, the plain-spoken turf-cutter; Clym's particular admirer, Humphrey, the furze-cutter; and Olly, the obsequious besom-maker. This chorus, as in stage tragedy, serves the purpose both of exposition and of dramatic irony. The latter function is evident in Chapter 5 of Book I when the heath-folk arrive at the inn to serenade Wildeve and Thomasin, whom they suppose to be married. As spokesman, Fairway then unconsciously stings the devious Wildeve twice; first by complimenting him on gaining a wife whose father 'always had his great indignation ready against anything underhand', and second by remarking that the man who gains Eustacia will 'have an uncommon picture for his best parlour'. Similarly, there is ironic misunderstanding when Clym attempts to explain himself to the chorus in the hair-cutting scene. However, the choral comments are often poignantly perceptive, as in Sam's verdict on Eustacia: 'I should rather say her thoughts were far away from here, with lords and ladies she'll never know, and mansions she'll never see again' (III:ii). Altogether, the choral parts recall the 'comic relief' of Elizabethan drama, the alternation of tragic and comic tone. In the very last chapter of the novel we find the 'Egdon coterie' stuffing a feather bed as a wedding present; and, though there is only a hint of ribaldry in this scene, it is perhaps not too far-fetched to recognize here a reminiscence of the satyr play which followed a performance of Greek tragedy.

Tragic Characterization in *The Return of the Native*

In the tragic context Hardy's characterization takes on added resonance, though of course it does not literally follow Aristotle's prescription that the protagonist be of noble family in order that his fall may be the more momentous. Yet, in the restricted social setting of Egdon, Clym and Eustacia are the highest in rank; as gentility here is the equivalent of nobility, Mrs Yeobright may appear as Clytemnestra, with a gulf fixed between her and the heath-folk. Aristotle also noted that the protagonist's fall or destruction is typically brought about not by evil disposition, but merely by some venial fault, blindness or misjudgement – the so-called 'tragic flaw'. Accordingly, Mrs Yeobright's flaw is the vehemence of her maternity. Clym's failings are complacency and a stubbornness that twice makes him fatally put off reconciliation. Eustacia is destroyed by discontent.

We can also recognize in Clym and Eustacia another quality associated with the tragic flaw, i.e. hubris, which has been traditionally understood as that presumption which attracts Nemesis. In the *Oresteia*, for example, Agamemnon shows hubris just before his murder by treading upon crimson coverings, an honour reserved for divinity. Eustacia tempts fate by 'pride in life' and by her prayer, so ironically answered, 'O . . . send me great love from somewhere, else I shall die' (I:vii). Both she and Clym are 'Promethean' in their presumption, inasmuch as they defy society and conventional morality for the sake of love, though Eustacia's ideal is passionate love and the exaltation of self, and Clym's, love of humanity and abnegation. The passion between them illustrates the danger of loving too deeply, of giving oneself over to celestial joy in a sublunary world. Thus in the eclipse scene on Rainbarrow – another example of 'dramatic' structure – in which the lovers exchange pledges in rhetorical speeches, Eustacia's irrepressible misgivings – 'They say such love never lasts' (III:iv) – are as ominous as Clym's blind optimism. Like Agamemnon in the grip of hubris, Hardy's lovers are fey; their actions and speech foreshadow doom. However, hubris becomes even more explicit elsewhere. Eustacia certainly shows it in her avowal of hatred for mankind and Nature; and Clym makes both Thomasin and Eustacia shudder by his ill-omened exclamation while mourning his mother: 'If [God] would only strike me with more pain I would believe in Him for ever!' (V:i).

Yet Hardy's tragedy is neither didactic nor moralistic. Its doomed protagonists are not held up as warning, for, in view of the antagonism of fate, hubris – the 'pride of life' – is inherent in all existence. The recognition of this universality is central in Hardy's evocation of 'pity and terror', the emotions which Aristotle identified as effecting tragic catharsis. Of particular relevance here is Hardy's own definition of tragedy, in a notebook entry of 1885, as 'a state of things in the life of an individual which unavoidably causes some natural aim or desire of his to end in a catastrophe when carried out'. From this perspective Clym's fatal return appears not as presumption, but as a natural act. Even Eustacia's ultimately destructive devotion to sexual passion partakes of this naturalness, as if Yeats's lines on Maud Gonne were written expressly for Hardy's heroine:

> Why, what could she have done, being what she is?
> Was there another Troy for her to burn?

> ('No Second Troy')

Mrs Yeobright wants her son, Eustacia wants love, Clym wants to do something meaningful; and all these natural motives are mainsprings of catastrophe.

Moreover, in keeping with Aristotle's observation that the tragic hero should be noble in character as well as in lineage, Hardy's protagonists are endowed with heroic stature. This exalted stature, which seems to be inseparable from the exhibition of hubris, is evident in Eustacia's 'grandeur of temper' and 'mind that, though disappointed, forswears compromise'. Indeed, Hardy invites comparison with Milton's Satan: 'A true Tartarean dignity sat upon [Eustacia's] brow' (I:vii); though flawed by meaner instincts, she is capable of courage, generosity and indignation. Clym's nobility is also sufficiently established, and it is emblematized in Eustacia's vision: 'Clym, the eclipsed moonlight shines upon your face with a strange foreign colour, and shows its shape as if it were cut out in gold' (III:iv). However, the fates of Clym and Eustacia express a 'modern' sense of tragedy in the incompatibility of life and virtue, whether we take virtue to be honour, dignity, feeling or idealism. The protagonists' proud refusal to propitiate fate or bow to its dictates is pointed up by the grovelling figure of Christian, who clings to a miserable existence in the dread of hell and the devil. Yet this heroism is inseparable from pathos and the sense of waste – the word 'waste' recurs thematically – the waste of Clym's promise, Eustacia's 'sad and stifled warmth' (I:vii). Laid out after drowning, even Wildeve looks as if 'born for a higher destiny than this' (V:ix). The incompatibility of life and virtue is powerfully symbolized in the very last, supremely ironic scene of Book V, in which Eustacia's greatest radiance is in death, the element which has forever chilled her warmth seeming momentarily to have enhanced it. This culminating *tableau* also realizes catharsis, as the anguish of Books IV and V is distilled into beauty and repose:

They stood silently looking upon Eustacia, who, as she lay there still in death, eclipsed all her living phases. Pallor did not include all the quality of her complexion, which seemed more than whiteness; it was almost light. The expression of her finely carved mouth was pleasant, as if a sense of dignity had just compelled her to leave off speaking. Eternal rigidity had seized upon it in a momentary transition between fervour and resignation. Her black hair was looser now than either of them had ever seen it before, and surrounded her brow like a forest. The stateliness of look which had been almost too marked for a dweller in a country domicile had at last found an artistically happy background.

(V:ix)

Concluding Book V, Clym speaks with apparent calmness of 'the horror of my existence'. Indeed, the protagonist's perception of that 'coil of things' inevitably distorting human life is central to the sense of tragedy in Hardy. Of course Eustacia also shows this brooding awareness of doom, while Thomasin and Venn are non-tragic characters in the sense that they, perhaps fortunately, lack tragic perception. 'Trouble has taught you a deeper vein of talk than mine' (V:ii), Venn tells Clym. Hardy ultimately saw tragedy as a philosophical statement about the nature of existence; and he came closest to a non-fictional articulation of this statement in his General Preface, in response to the critics who attacked his pessimism:

It must be obvious that there is a higher characteristic of philosophy than pessimism, or than meliorism, or even than the optimism of these critics – which is truth. Existence is either ordered in a certain way, or it is not so ordered, and conjectures which harmonize best with experience are removed above all comparison with other conjectures which do not so harmonize.

Thus, for Hardy, tragedy is testimony to a higher realism; it is a vision of life both instinctive in us – what 'Aeschylus imagined our nursery children feel' – and harmonious with experience.

However, in modern times Hardy's portrayal of tragedy in *The Return* has been criticized not so much for 'pessimism', as for inconsistency or confusion. Some readers have found the classical allusions and parallels obtrusive, or they have been bothered by the narrator's portentous tone, which sometimes seems ill-suited to the characters' more mundane actions and speech. Eustacia's petulance to Clym falls short of 'grandeur of temper': 'Dearest, you must not question me unpleasantly, or it may make me not love you' (IV:ii). When such inconsistencies become apparent, we must admit Hardy's failure fully to resolve the simultaneity of realistic and tragic levels of plot and character. At the same time, the appearance of mundaneness or pettiness in the protagonists may reflect Hardy's intention to show the diminishment of humanity in a tragic universe, i.e. the 'overpowering of the fervid by the inanimate' (V:iii). In the scene of Clym's tragic frenzy following his discovery, 'the imperturbable countenance of the heath . . . reduced to insignificance by its seamed and antique features the wildest turmoil of a single man' (V:ii). By obliging Hardy to portray post-catastrophic scenes, Book VI introduced further potential for inconsistency; here, indeed, the conflict of novel form and tragic form is apparent. These inconsistencies in form and characterization have caused critics to rank *The Return* a degree lower than his other great tragic novels, which do not attempt to preserve the Aristotelian unities. With respect to the achievement of tragic heroism, we too must admit that Clym and Eustacia fall short of Tess and Henchard in *The Mayor of Casterbridge*, both of whom are destroyed but not defeated by fate.

The Mythic Level of Plot

We conclude our study of *The Return* with a survey of the mythic structure underlying the action. This level may be said to be irrational in the sense that its coherence is based on thought associations or mystic correspondences, rather than on the Aristotelian logic of plot. Accordingly, the mythic level is the province of symbols, dreams, ritual or symbolic action, and unconscious allegory, insofar as these reflect primal, universal patterns. At this level both the realistic and tragic plots merge into archetypes of Western literature and culture. The mythic level of literature may be 'unconscious' in the sense either that the author does not acknowledge his use of mythic material or that he himself is not fully aware of the relation of this material to archetypal patterns. Arguably, we find both kinds of unconsciousness in *The Return*, in addition to conscious evocations of myth as in the repeated allusions to Prometheus, the archetypal defier of omnipotence, or the reference to Oedipus, who, like Prometheus, is both a mythic figure and a tragic hero.

Let us look first at Hardy's overt use of myth. His more obvious symbols (e.g. the hourglass, holly, the adder) certainly draw attention to a mythic dimension, and other objects are frequently transfigured by a fetishistic power. Thus the turf-cutter 'carried across his shoulder the singular heart-shaped spade of large dimensions used in that species of labour, and its well-whetted edge gleamed like a silver bow in the beams of the fire' (I:iii). The narrator, in his role as interpreter, repeatedly reminds us that culture and the mind, like the landscape, are palimpsests with hidden primitive or pagan layers. The branding of Eustacia as a witch 'was one of those sentiments which lurk like moles underneath the visible surface of manners' (V:ii). We are expressly invited to consider the mythological background of folklore; to look upon customs such as the Guy Fawkes bonfire or the mumming as re-enactments of the ancient past. In the bonfire scene on Rainbarrow:

It was as if these men and boys had suddenly dived into past ages, and fetched therefrom an hour and deed which had before been familiar with this spot. The ashes of the original British pyre which blazed from that summit lay fresh and undisturbed in the barrow beneath their tread. The flames from funeral piles long ago kindled there had shone down upon the lowlands as these were shining now.

Festival fires to Thor and Woden had followed on the same ground and duly had their day. Indeed, it is pretty well known that such blazes as this the heathmen were now enjoying are rather the lineal descendants from jumbled Druidical rites and Saxon ceremonies than the invention of popular feeling about Gunpowder Plot.

Moreover to light a fire is the instinctive and resistant act of man when, at the winter ingress, the curfew is sounded throughout Nature. It indicates a spontaneous, Promethean rebelliousness against the fiat that this recurrent season shall bring foul times, cold darkness, misery and death. Black chaos comes, and the fettered gods of the earth say, Let there be light.

(I:iii)

We have already spoken of the heath-folk as forming, on the tragic level, a chorus; but in this bonfire scene we seem to see them, on the mythic level, as a ritual group. The mumming scenes give a similar impression of the performance of communal rite.

However, in addition to this explicit or conscious use of myth, Hardy also exploits it in an 'unconscious' manner inasmuch as the mythic correspondences may be unacknowledged or hidden. As such, they echo subconsciously in the reader's mind until attention is drawn to them and they become obvious. An example is the intimation of the Garden of Eden myth. There are various unobtrusive allusions to Adam and Eden, in addition to Christian's fearful recollection of 'the old serpent in God's garden, that gied the apple to the young woman with no clothes' (IV:vii). Moreover, Wildeve is likened to Satan as the tempter of Eve in *Paradise Lost*; Venn, to the angel Ithuriel, who in Milton's epic detects Satan in his first penetration, in the guise of a toad, of Eden. Finally, in the scene of Mrs Yeobright's fatal arrival at Alderworth, we see a lone apple tree in the garden, its fruit fallen and spoiled, while the tempter is within the precincts. Another example of implicit correspondence is that of Clym with Christ. As Adam, Clym is already, theologically, a type of Christ. But we also have Clym's fame as a twelve-year-old prodigy, his preference of his mission to his mother, his preaching of spiritual integrity over material gain, his rising from apparent death, his 'Sermons on the Mount' at the age of not quite thirty-three, and his final role of redeemer and scapegoat.

Hardy's most casual or obscure allusions usually reward analysis. An especially intriguing example is Johnny Nunsuch's question to Mrs Yeobright as she retreats in horror from Clym's door: 'What have made you so down? Have you seen a ooser?' (IV:vi). Few of Hardy's original readers could have known that the dialect word 'ooser' denotes a fearsome mask in the shape of a horned bull's head. Such a mask, a remarkably primitive survival in nineteenth-century Dorset, was worn by mummers, by the impersonator of the cuckold in a 'skimmity-riding' (I:v), by pranksters and, supposedly, by witches. The ooser image, then, focuses several folklore themes. The witchcraft association comes first to mind, both Johnny and Mrs Yeobright having seen Eustacia's apparently malign face staring from the window. In view of the association with skimmity-riding, a traditional pillorying of adultery, the ooser also raises the spectre of Clym's apparent cuckoldry. But deeper still in the collective unconscious, the ooser represents the potent and immemorially ancient horned-beast dancer, the ooser-wearing mummers of Hardy's childhood having their prototype in Neolithic cave paintings. For a classically-educated person, the ooser also recalls the Minotaur, the bull-headed monster to whom youths and maidens were sacrificed. In fact, Eustacia's sinister dream of dancing with a masked partner, which prefigures her own and Wildeve's deaths in the 'boiling cauldron', has already been likened to the 'Cretan labyrinth' (II:iii). Was Hardy, then, imagining Eustacia and Wildeve as the devoted victims of a horned Moloch?

Such a question can be answered only generally, in the affirmation that human sacrifice does indeed seem to be at the basis of the mythic plot. To recapitulate, we assume that at the mythic level the author himself is not fully aware of the archetypes which his narrative exploits; that the evocative power of these archetypes is exerted in the mutual unconsciousness of author and reader – the full implications of the ooser image, for example, would be apparent only to a folklorist. Consequently, statements of Hardy's intentions in the mythic plot must remain incomplete and ambiguous. Here we may pose two more unanswerable questions. Did Hardy, while writing *The Return*, intuit the theory, later elaborated by the Cambridge school of anthropology, that ancient tragedy originated in autumn rituals of human sacrifice, the victim evolving into the tragic protagonist? Again, did Hardy realize that in the mummers' *Play of St George*, with which he counterpointed his tragic plot, he was dealing with a vestigial transition stage between ritual and drama?

Eustacia as Mythic Victim

With these limitations and uncertainties in mind, let us proceed to our analysis of the mythic plot. As already intimated, this plot centres on Eustacia's role as a sacrificial victim, a role which we may approach through its link to the witchcraft theme. At the realistic level, Eustacia's physical darkness and 'saturnine' personality naturally attract vulgar suspicions of witchcraft. She herself is unaware of her 'magic reputation', though she compares herself to the Witch of Endor, whom Saul consulted, in her triumph at having 'called up' Wildeve to her bonfire. However, on the 'unconscious' level, symbols and motifs of sorcery cluster about Eustacia; and this pattern becomes more striking when we recall that in the Ur-novel she had been a witch in fact. Relevant symbols here include her hourglass (traditionally associated with selling one's soul, and carried by the devil in *The Woodlanders*), the crooked sixpence (a charm against witchcraft) with which she rewards Johnny for stoking her fire, and the flint arrowheads (called in dialect 'elf-shots' and known as the ammunition of sorcery) which Charley collects for her. The frogs appear to be her familiars; Johnny thinks 'she charmed 'en to come' (I:viii). As hinted by the allusion to the Witch of Endor, an act of necromancy is shadowed in Eustacia's 'calling up' of Wildeve. Such an act might require an innocent's sacrifice; indeed, Johnny is peakish ever after attending Eustacia's fire.

Like frogs, serpents too would be a witch's agents; certainly, the adder-stung Mrs Yeobright dies the moment Eustacia appears at the turf-shed. In that scene the supernatural has already been implicated when an adder captured for use in the homeopathic folk remedy for snakebite confronts the stricken woman: 'Mrs Yeobright saw the creature, and the creature saw her: she quivered throughout, and averted her eyes.' At this, Christian mutters, ' 'Tis to be hoped [the adder] can't ill-wish us! There's folks in heath who've been overlooked already' (IV:vii). Now, in dialect, to 'overlook' is to blast with the evil eye; and the adder's eyeing of Mrs Yeobright reminds us of Eustacia's stare at her mother-in-law from the overlooking window. Etymologically, 'fascinate', another word associated with Eustacia, also means to bewitch; and Clym's 'fascination' reaches its climax under a lunar eclipse, traditionally the most favourable time for the casting of spells. No wonder, in their confrontation, Clym rebukes Eustacia, 'Don't look at me with those eyes as if you would bewitch me again!' (V:iii).

Thus Hardy deliberately establishes Eustacia's witch persona on the subliminal level. Here her Satanic character underlies her reign as 'Queen of Night' as well as her Promethean refusal to bow to God's will. In her figurative enmity to light, Eustacia is also Lilith, 'Adam's first wife . . . (The witch he loved before the gift of Eve,)' – in the words of Rossetti's sonnet on his painting *Lady Lilith* (1864). This archetypal antithesis of Lilith and Eve underlies Hardy's use of the convention of paired dark and light heroines; and a Manichaean conflict between darkness and light, or between body and soul, is also vaguely implicit in the antithesis between Eustacia and Thomasin.

Yet this demonic aspect of Eustacia does not prevent her being herself a victim, a role which, on the evidence of the Ur-novel, she usurped from Thomasin. Subliminally a witch, Eustacia is also a victim of sorcery, both literally and figuratively. Pricking with a bodkin, which Susan inflicts upon Eustacia as a magical counteraction of her spells, had been a method of torment used by Renaissance witch-hunters. Similarly, the words 'faggot', 'stake' and 'bonfire', which recur in the Guy Fawkes scene on Rainbarrow, connote witch-burning. The grim etymology of 'bonfire' is 'bone fire'; and just as the 'mommet', or guy, is burnt on Rainbarrow, Eustacia herself is burnt in effigy a year later by Susan. Presumably, Eustacia would have been burnt literally had she lived at the time of her fifteenth-century Dorset namesake. Moreover, the rope burn which she suffers on her hand is perhaps a reminiscence of the ordeal of 'witch-swimming', in which a suspected witch, bound hand and foot, was drawn on a rope through water (a weir-pool is used for this purpose in Ainsworth's *Lancashire Witches*). If the victim floated, her guilt was proven. But, by the terms of this ordeal, Eustacia's innocence is finally vindicated, for the water of the weir does not refuse to close over her.

Behind this figure of the persecuted witch, however, we can recognize that of the victim of ritual sacrifice, the archetypal victim symbolized by Guy Fawkes. In her dream Eustacia is the chosen partner of a mysterious masquer, and the meaning of their pairing is revealed when we finally see her displayed, in her greatest beauty, as the bride of death. Of course, we also see Eustacia slain in ritual combat by St George; and this mummers' play, according to modern folklorists, is a superficially Christianized descendant of ancient rites in which a human victim was put to death, both as a purificatory scapegoat and as a representative either of the waning year or of winter. Evidently, in Hardy's version of the play, the Turkish Knight stands for this ritual victim, while the victorious St George is the disguised representative either of the waxing year or of summer. Although Hardy could scarcely have been aware of this underlying seasonal myth, his narrative is instinctively organized into seasonal divisions marked by four distinct rituals – the Guy Fawkes commemoration in autumn, the mumming at the winter solstice, the Maypoling in spring, and the 'gipsying' in summer, though spring is displaced to the end of the cycle. Intriguingly, just as the ancient autumn rite of sacrifice was accompanied by fertility dances, Hardy's heath-folk spontaneously dance in the embers of the fire in which they have burnt the guy; and they then proceed to a wedding serenade.

In this context Eustacia's uncanny, dark beauty marks her as one devoted to death. Moreover, her moral character is fitting to her mythic role. By her unconcealed antipathy to Nature, God and her fellow men, she has set herself apart. This apartness from the community, an isolation that would have been fatal in witch-hunting times, is underscored by her admiration for Napoleon, who, as 'Boney', was a Wessex folk demon. It has also been pointed out that her kindling of a private fire on Guy Fawkes Day is a kind of sacrilege, an unforgivable violation of communal rite. Eustacia, then, is an obvious scapegoat, a natural victim of the communal reprobation expressed in Susan's symbolic burning of her. At the same time, Eustacia's character as a chosen victim sharply contrasts with that of Clym, who, like Christ, is willing to sacrifice himself for the good of the community. Yet it is apparently Eustacia's death which is demanded and which, by the logic of the mythic plot, makes possible the renewal of life. Certainly, the catastrophe is followed by the Maypoling and wedding of Book VI, just as a performance of Greek tragedy was followed by a satyr play, i.e. a disguised fertility rite.

In her ritual death as the Turkish Knight, Eustacia sinks slowly to the floor under St George's blows. This gradual fall recurs in her last living appearance, on Rainbarrow, where – while her effigy is slowly burning in Susan's fire – we see Eustacia 'gradually crouching down . . . as if she were being drawn into the Barrow by a hand from beneath' (V:vii). Thus her martyrdom becomes continuous with the immolations of antiquity, as does that of Tess, whom we last see lying upon the Stone of Sacrifice at Stonehenge as the sun rises. This half-conscious sense of mythic re-enactment endows Hardy's protagonists with a unique and scarcely definable profundity.

Bibliography

Editions

The Return of the Native, introduction by Albert J. Guerard (Holt, Rinehart, 1950).

The Return of the Native, introduction and notes by Derwent May (Macmillan, 1974).

The Return of the Native, introduction and notes by George Woodcock (Penguin, 1978).

Biography

ROBERT GITTINGS, *The Older Hardy* (Penguin, 1980).

ROBERT GITTINGS, *Young Thomas Hardy* (Penguin, 1978).

FLORENCE EMILY HARDY, *The Life of Thomas Hardy* [actually Hardy's autobiography] (Macmillan, 1962).

MICHAEL MILLGATE, *Thomas Hardy: A Biography* (Oxford University Press, 1982).

RICHARD LITTLE PURDY and MICHAEL MILLGATE, *The Collected Letters of Thomas Hardy* (Clarendon Press, 1978).

CARL J. WEBER, *Hardy of Wessex* (Columbia University Press, 1965).

Criticism

RICHARD BENVENUTO, 'The Return of the Native as a Tragedy in Six Books', *Nineteenth-Century Fiction* (June 1971).

PETER J. CASAGRANDE, *Unity in Hardy's Novels* (Macmillan, 1982).

R. G. COX (ed.), *Thomas Hardy: The Critical Heritage* [reprints first reviews of *The Return*] (Routledge & Kegan Paul, 1970).

LEONARD DEEN, 'Heroism and Pathos in *The Return of the Native*', *Nineteenth-Century Fiction* (December 1960).

R. P. DRAPER (ed.), *Hardy: The Tragic Novels: A Casebook* (Macmillan, 1975).

RUTH A. FIROR, *Folkways in Thomas Hardy* (University of Pennsylvania Press, 1931).

NORTHROP FRYE, *Anatomy of Criticism* (Princeton University Press, 1957).

ELLIOTT B. GOSE, JR, *Imagination Indulged: The Irrational in the Nineteenth-Century Novel* (McGill–Queen's University Press, 1972).

IAN GREGOR, *The Great Web: The Form of Hardy's Major Fiction* (Faber & Faber, 1974).

Critical Studies: The Return of the Native

DALE KRAMER, *Thomas Hardy: The Forms of Tragedy* (Macmillan, 1975).

DALE KRAMER, 'Unity of Time in *The Return of the Native*', *Notes and Queries* (August 1965).

D. H. LAWRENCE, 'Study of Thomas Hardy', *Phoenix* (Heinemann, 1936).

J. HILLIS MILLER, *Thomas Hardy: Distance and Desire* (Oxford University Press, 1970).

MICHAEL MILLGATE, *Thomas Hardy: His Career as a Novelist* (Bodley Head, 1971).

ROY MORRELL, *Thomas Hardy: The Will and the Way* (University of Malaya Press, 1965).

JOHN PATERSON, *The Making of 'The Return of the Native'* (University of California Press, 1960).

JOHN PATERSON, '*The Return of the Native* as Antichristian Document', *Nineteenth-Century Fiction* (September 1959).

JOHN R. REED, *Victorian Conventions* (Ohio State University Press, 1975).

LAWRENCE J. STARZYK, 'The Coming Universal Wish not to Live in Hardy's "Modern" Novels', *Nineteenth-Century Fiction* (March 1972).

HARVEY CURTIS WEBSTER, *On a Darkling Plain: The Art and Thought of Thomas Hardy* (University of Chicago Press, 1947).

OTIS B. WHEELER, 'Four Versions of *The Return of the Native*', *Nineteenth-Century Fiction* (June 1959).

VIRGINIA WOOLF, 'The Novels of Thomas Hardy', *The Common Reader* (Hogarth Press, 1932).

KEN ZELLEFROW, 'Hardy's Map and Eustacia's Suicide', *Nineteenth-Century Fiction* (September 1973).